300

Three Minute Games

Quick and Easy Activities
For 2-5 Year Olds

By Jackie Silberg

Illustrations by Cheryl Kirk Noll

gryphon house

Beltsville, Maryland

Other books by Jackie Silberg available from
Gryphon House

Games to Play with Babies
Games to Play with Toddlers
Games to Play with Two Year Olds
More Games to Play with Toddlers
500 Five Minute Games

Copyright © 1997 Jackie Silberg
Published by Gryphon House, Inc.
10726 Tucker Street, Beltsville MD 20705

World Wide Web: http://wwwghbooks.com

The author of this book, Jackie Silberg, is an acclaimed speaker, teacher and trainer
on early childhood development and music. You can arrange to have her speak,
present, train or entertain by contacting her through Gryphon House, PO Box 207,
Beltsville MD 20704-0207 or at jsilberg@interserv.com.

Cover Design: Lightbourne Images
Text Illustrations: Cheryl Kirk Noll

Library of Congress Cataloging-in-Publication Data

Silberg, Jackie, 1934-

     300 three minute games : quick and easy activities for 2-5 year
olds / Jackie Silberg : illustrations by Cheryl Kirk Noll.
     p.   cm.
     Includes index.
     ISBN 0-87659-182-9
     1. Games. 2. Rhyming games. I. Noll, Cheryl Kirk. II. Title.
GV 1203. S534 1997   98-37864
792--dc21   CIP

Contents

● ●

Introduction

● ●

Taking the time to play with a child is a gift for yourself as well as a gift for the child. This book is full of stimulating games that challenge the imagination and are developmentally appropriate for young children. There are waiting games for when you are stuck in traffic, story games to build language skills, exercise games, stuffed animal games and quiet games. Use these short creative activities to delight and teach children whenever you need to fill an extra few minutes or any time just for fun. I hope that by using this book your days will be more delightful as you spend time with cherished children.

I would like to dedicate this book to all the children I have had the good fortune to play with, learn from and enjoy over the years.

I am also deeply indebted to Kathy Charner, my editor, whose intelligent and thoughtful comments support me.

Finally, to Leah Curry-Rood and Larry Rood, owners of Gryphon House, who deeply care about young children and are always an inspiration.

Jackie Silberg

Animal Games

I'm an Animal
● ●

Teaches about animals

▲ Pretend to be an animal, for example, a rabbit.
▲ Hop back and forth like a rabbit.
▲ Give your child directions to hop to different places, such as hop to the chair, hop to the door.
▲ Give your child a carrot to eat while she is pretending to be a rabbit.
▲ Choose other animals: a fish can swim and drink water, a duck can waddle and quack.

Billy Is a Blue Bird
● ●

Teaches about animals

▲ Sing the following to the tune of "Mary Had a Little Lamb":

> *Billy is a blue bird,*
> *Blue bird, blue bird.*
> *Billy is a blue bird*
> *Fly, fly away.*

▲ Spread your arms out and show Billy how to fly.
▲ Sing other verses. Change the animal and the color each time.

> *Billy is a brown snake....*
> *Billy is a yellow duck....*
> *Billy is a purple cow....*

Dog Named Rover
● ●

Encourages bonding

▲ Ask your child to lie on her back.

▲ Say the poem and do the following actions:

> As I was walking down the street,
>   *(move child's legs back and forth)*
> I saw a dog named Rover.
> "Come here, Rover and play with me,
>   *(move child's hands in beckoning motion)*
> And then we'll both turn over."
>   *(turn over)*

ANIMAL GAMES

Little Birdie

Promotes bonding

▲ This poem has a happy ending. Say it once, then do the actions with your child.

> What does the little birdie say
> In her nest at the peak of day?
> "Let me fly," says the birdie, (child flaps arms like a flying bird)
> "Mother, please let me fly."
> "Birdie dear, rest a little longer (child sits down)
> 'Till your little wings are stronger."
> So she rests and rests all day
> Then she wakes and flies away. (child flaps arms like a bird flying)

The Kitty Game

Promotes coordination

▲ Say the following poem and encourage your child to do the actions.
▲ Make a fist with your right hand.
▲ Take the thumb of your right hand, wiggle it and say, "Meow, meow."
▲ Put your thumb inside the fist of your other hand.

> Where is kitty? He's not at home.
> Is kitty out in the back yard playing with some yarn?
> Is kitty hiding behind the sofa?
> Come on out kitty, please
> Meow, meow, meow. (bring out thumb from inside fist)

Little Kitty
•••••••••••••••••••••••••••

Promotes coordination

▲ Take the pointer finger of one hand and touch the fingers and thumb of the other hand.

▲ Start with the little finger.

> This little kitty lost her sweater.
> This little kitty lost her muff.
> This little kitty said, "It's cold outside."
> This little kitty said, "Ooooh, look at that white stuff."
> This little kitty said, "Brrreeeee,
> This nice warm house is the place for me."
> (put your thumb in your fist)

▲ Encourage your child to do this fingerplay with you.

Frogs
•••••••••••••••••••••••••••

Encourages coordination

▲ Young children love to jump. It's a major accomplishment for them.

▲ Jump to the following poem:

> Frogs jump high
> Up to the sky.
> Frogs jump low
> To and fro.
> Jump little frog
> Faster, faster.
> Jump little frog
> And...splash! (pretend to fall in the water)

> Jackie Silberg

Leap Frog

Develops coordination

▲ Pretend to be a frog. Show your child how frogs hop about.
▲ Put a stuffed animal on the floor and jump over it.
▲ Ask your child to copy you.
▲ Help your child bend down and hop over the stuffed animal.

Be a Butterfly

Builds coordination

▲ Sit on the floor and put the soles of your feet together.
▲ Move your knees up and down like they are wings.
▲ Say, "Butterfly, butterfly, let's fly!"
▲ Bring your arms up over your head and let them flutter as you move your knees up and down.
▲ Say, "Butterfly, let's land."
▲ Let your hands come to rest on your feet.
▲ Encourage your child to copy your movements.

Ants

● ●

Builds counting skills

▲ Say the poem and do the actions. Help your child to close his hand into a fist with his thumb tucked into the fist.

> Once I saw an ant hill (make a fist with thumb in)
> With no ants about.
> So I said, "Dear little ants
> Won't you please come out?"
> Then as if the little ants
> Heard my little shout,
> One, two, three, four, five (open up fist one finger at a time)
> They all came out.

Way Up in the Sky

● ●

Develops creativity

▲ This poem encourages children to act out the story and pretend to be birds.

> Way up in the sky
> The little birdies fly. (pretend to fly)
> Way down in their nest
> The little birdies rest. (pretend to rest)
> With a wing on the right, (flap right arm)
> And a wing on the left, (flap left arm)
> The sweet little birdies
> Sleep in their nest. (pretend to sleep)
> The bright sun comes up, (circle arms like the sun)
> The dew fades away, (flutter fingers downward)
> "Good morning, good morning,"
> The little birdies say.

Galloping
● ●

Teaches about fast and slow

▲ Gallop around the room with your child and say the rhyme. For the first verse say the words and move quickly; for the second verse say the words and move slowly.

> Galloping, galloping all around.
> Galloping, galloping, down to town.
> Faster, faster, don't be late
> Galloping to the garden gate.
>
> Galloping, galloping, home again.
> Slowly, slowly, home again.
> Gall-op-ing, gall-op-ing
> Home.... (sit down and pretend to fall asleep)

Jackie Silberg

Itty Bitty Kitty
● ●

Develops imagination

▲ Pretend to be a kitty and crawl on the floor and say, "Meow."
▲ Say to your child, "Come here itty bitty kitty."
▲ Have your child come to you and say, "Meow, meow."
▲ Pet your itty bitty kitty and say, "What a nice kitty."
▲ You can extend this game in many ways. Ask the kitty to roll over, wag her tail or go to sleep.

Gorillas

●●●●●●●●●●●●●●●●●●●●●●●●●●●●●●●●

Develops imagination

▲ Show your child how to walk like a gorilla.
▲ Spread your feet apart and bend your body forward. Let your arms swing freely.
▲ Take slow, plodding steps, swinging your arms from side to side.
▲ Walk around the room making gorilla sounds.

Elephant Hunt

●●●●●●●●●●●●●●●●●●●●●●●●●●●●●●●●

Develops imagination

▲ Talk about how elephants like to eat peanuts.
▲ Show your child how to walk like an elephant and pretend that your arms are the trunk.
▲ Hide some peanuts in your house or outside.
▲ Walk like an elephant and look for the peanuts.
▲ Show your child how to take off the shell. This is a good way to exercise finger muscles and develop coordination.
▲ You could play this same game pretending to be a squirrel who has hidden nuts for the winter.

ANIMAL GAMES

Doggie Chase
● ●

Develops imagination

▲ Get down on your knees and pretend to be a dog.
▲ Move forward and bark.
▲ Move backward and bark.
▲ Chase your child as you bark like a dog.
▲ Try to do some doggie tricks. Ask your child to give the commands and you obey, such as sit, heel.
▲ This is a lot of fun, especially for your child.

Be a Monkey
● ●

Encourages imagination

▲ Before you play this game, show your child pictures of monkeys or visit a zoo where she can watch monkeys.
▲ Pretend to be a monkey climbing a tree. Make a monkey sound, such as chee, chee.
▲ Say the following poem as you pretend to be monkeys:

Monkey in the tree
Swinging all around.
Jump from branch to branch
Ooops, you fell down. (tumble to
the ground)

Five Little Monkeys

Teaches jumping skills

▲ Hold your child's hand as you say the following rhyme and do the actions:

> Five little monkeys jumping on the bed. (hold hands and jump up and down)
> One fell down and hurt his little head. (fall to the ground and pretend to cry)
> Mama called the doctor and the doctor said, (pretend to call on a phone)
> "No more monkeys jumping on the bed." (shake your index finger)

▲ Ask your child, "Can you jump like a little monkey?"

Charley Barley

Teaches language skills

▲ This is a great poem to act out. Pretend to be a duck and at the end of the poem fly away.

> Charley Barley, butter and eggs
> Sold his car for three duck eggs.
>   (hold up three fingers)
> When the ducks began to lay
> Charley Barley flew away.
>   (fly around the room)

Gobble, Quack
• •

Develops language skills

▲ Talk about animal sounds. Make the sounds of two animals, for example a turkey and a duck.

▲ Say the following poem:

> *Gobble, gobble, gobble*
> *Quack, quack, quack*
> *Turkeys go gobble*
> *And ducks quack, quack.*

▲ If you are playing this game with more than two people (you and a child) let the next person say two animal sounds, for example, "Moo" and "Meow."

▲ Say the poem again.

> *Moo, moo, moo*
> *Meow, meow, meow*
> *Cows go moo and*
> *Cats meow.*

▲ Keep adding animal sounds.

Here's a Fish

●●●●●●●●●●●●●●●●●●●●●●●●●●

Develops language skills

▲ If your child has seen pictures of fish or visited an aquarium, this game will be more meaningful.

▲ Pour crackers shaped like fish into a bowl.

▲ Pick up a cracker and sing the following to the tune of "The Muffin Man":

> *Oh, do you know this little fish,*
> *This little fish, this little fish.*
> *Oh, do you know this little fish*
> *It swims around and 'round.*

▲ As you sing the song, move the cracker around and around and on the last word pop it into your mouth.

▲ Your child will want to do it too.

ANIMAL GAMES

Animal Songs

•••••••••••••••••••••••••••••

▲ Children are particularly fond of songs, games and books about animals.

▲ The more that you sing with your child, the more his language skills will develop, which include speaking and reading.

▲ Here are a few songs about animals. Can you think of more?

"Itsy Bitsy Spider"
"Five Little Ducks"
"Old MacDonald Had a Farm"
"All the Fish"
"Shoo Fly"
"Bing-O"

Animal Moves

•••••••••••••••••••••••••••••

Enhances listening skills

▲ Say the rhyme and do the actions.

Let's hop, hop, hop like a bunny.
Let's run, run, run like a dog.
Let's walk, walk, walk like an elephant.
And jump, jump, jump like a frog.
Let's swim, swim, swim like a fish.
And fly, fly, fly like a bird.
Now let's stop and sit right down,
And not say a single word.

Bath Games

This Little Pig
● ●

Develops bonding

▲ Say this traditional English rhyme at bath time.

> This little pig had a rub-a-dub-dub. (wash one leg)
> This little pig had a scrub-a-scrub-scrub. (wash the other leg)
> This little pig ran upstairs. (run your fingers up child's arm)
> This little pig called out, "Teddy bear."
>   (say the words in a big voice)
> Down came a jar with a great big slam.
>   (slap your hands on the water)
> And this little piggy ate all of the jam.
> Yum, yum, yum. (rub your child's tummy)

Hot Water, Cold Water
● ●

Promotes bonding

▲ Bath time is always a wonderful time for one-on-one interaction.
▲ Say, "Hot water, hot water, watch out, watch out."
▲ As you say these words, tap your child's shoulder with each syllable.
▲ Then say, "Cold water, cold water, running down your back." Tickle down her back.
▲ Once you have played the game, you can try squishing water from a washcloth down her back while saying, "Cold water, cold water."

Get Me Clean

●●●●●●●●●●●●●●●●●●●●●●●●●●●●●●●

Encourages bonding

▲ Say the following rhyme while giving your child a bath:

> *Washcloth, washcloth, get me clean. (change your voice)*
> *Where do you want to be clean? (back to first voice)*
> *I want to have my toesies clean. (change to "washcloth voice")*
> *I'm gonna get those toesies clean. (back to first voice)*

▲ Repeat the first two lines then change to a different part of the body on the last two lines.

▲ Soon your child will be saying the verse and telling you what part of her body she wants you to clean.

Pass the Shoe

• •

Teaches cooperation

▲ This is a good game to play when getting undressed for a bath.

▲ Sing the following song to the tune of "London Bridge":

> You can pass the shoe to me
> Shoe to me, shoe to me.
> You can pass the shoe to me
> Because it is bath time.

▲ Ask for the next article of clothing and incorporate it into the song as follows:

> You can pass the sock to me....
> You can pass the shirt to me....
> You can pass the pants to me....

Which Way

• •

Improves coordination

▲ This game is a lot of fun to play in the bathtub because the boat usually floats away and has to be retrieved.

▲ Take a toy boat or anything that will float.

▲ Ask your child to put the boat in front of her.

▲ Then ask her to put the boat on the side and in back of her.

▲ Ask your child to push the boat forward.

▲ Ask her to push the boat backward.

All the Fish

Develops coordination

▲ Put a very small amount of water in the bathtub.

▲ Have your child lie on her tummy and pretend to be a fish.

All the fish are swimming in the water
Swimming in the water, swimming in the water.
  (child pretends to swim)
All the fish are swimming in the water
Bubble, bubble, bubble, bubble, SPLASH!
  (splash the water)

▲ Pretend to be other things that swim in the water, such as ducks, tadpoles, frogs.

One O'Clock

Teaches counting skills

▲ This is a fun game to play in the bathtub. As you say the numbers, tap different parts of your child's body, such as bottoms of feet, tummy, top of head.

One o'clock, two o'clock, three o'clock, four
Who's that tapping at my door?
It's me, it's me with a great big kiss. (kiss child)

Five o'clock, six o'clock, seven o'clock, eight
It's me, it's me, now don't be late. (kiss child again)

Nine o'clock, ten
Let's do it again.

▲ Start at the beginning and repeat.

Sailing

Teaches about floating

▲ Tape half of a straw to the inside of an empty margarine container.

▲ Tie a ribbon to the straw or make a flag out of cardboard. Cut out a triangle and tape it to the straw.

▲ Put the boat in the bathtub and sing "Row, Row, Row Your Boat."

▲ Let your sailor play with the boat. Show him how to put toys in it to make it sink.

After the Bath
● ●

Encourages fun

▲ This is a good game to play while you dry your child.
▲ Say the words and do the actions.

> After a bath, I try, try, try
> To wipe myself dry, dry, dry.
> Hands to wipe and fingers and toes
> Two wet legs and a shiny nose.
> Think how much less time I'd take
> If I were a dog and could shake, shake, shake.

Here's Some Soup
● ●

Develops imagination

▲ Bath time is always very special. Most young children could stay in the bath forever.
▲ Pretend to make soup with your child. Put in the vegetables. Put in pretend carrots, onions, celery. Whatever you child suggests, accept them and say things, such as "What a good idea" or "That will make the soup taste yummy."
▲ Stir the soup with your hands.
▲ Pretend to serve and eat the soup.

Note: Do not drink the bath water.

Bath Toys

● ●

Develops imagination

▲ You can help develop your child's imagination while she is taking a bath.

▲ The bathtub is a good place to play with toy people.

▲ Stand a toy person on the end of the tub and say, "Ready, set, go! Dive in the water!"

▲ Take the toy and dive it into the water. Bring the toy up to the surface and have it swim to the side.

▲ This will encourage your child to do the same and make up her own ideas as well.

Eeny Meeny

● ●

Practices language skills

▲ Say the following nursery rhyme while giving your child a bath:

> *Eeny, meeny, miney mo*
> *Catch a tiger by the toe.*
> *If he hollers, let him go*
> *Eeny, meeny, miney mo.*

▲ On the words, "If he hollers, let him go" show your child how to holler. Use words that start with beginning vowel sounds like "aaaah" or "ooooooh."

▲ Say the poem again and wait for the holler before you say the last line of "Eeny, meeny, miney mo."

Rain Fun

Teaches language skills

▲ When you are finished with a yogurt or cottage cheese container, punch small holes in the bottom of it.

▲ Put it in the bathtub, scoop water into it, hold it up and watch the water come out of the holes.

▲ Sing the following song about rain as you do this:

> *Rain, rain, go away*
> *Come again another day.*
> *(Child's name) wants to play.*

▲ Other songs include:
"It's Raining, It's Pouring"
"Eensy, Weensy Spider"

Dressing

● ●

Encourages language skills

▲ Getting dressed after a bath or undressed before a bath is a perfect time to talk about clothes and where they belong.

▲ Say the name of each piece of clothing as you dress. "Your pants go on your legs. Then your shirt goes over your head."

▲ Continue naming each item: socks, shoes, etc.

▲ When you are finished dressing or undressing, sing the following song to the tune of "Are You Sleeping?":

> *We are dressing, we are dressing.*
> *Now we're through, now we're through.*
> *You look warm and clean, you look warm and clean.*
> *Hip, hooray, hip, hooray.*

Here Comes the Rain

● ●

Promotes observation skills

▲ This rhyme shows how you can feel water in different ways.

> *Here comes the rain,*
> *Splash, splash, splash. (splash the tub water)*
> *Here comes the rain*
> *Drip, drip, drip. (drip droplets of water on your child)*
> *Here comes the rain*
> *Pitter, patter. (flick your fingers in the water)*
> *Wash the child clean all over. (wash your child with a cloth)*

The Ice Cube Game
•••••••••••••••••••••••••••

Teaches about parts of the body

▲ This is a great bathtub game because you can put the ice cubes in the water when you are through and watch them melt.

▲ Put a few ice cubes in an ice bucket (or a bowl) and take them to the bathtub.

▲ Take an ice cube and rub it on your hand. Ask your child if she would like you to rub it on her hand.

▲ Ask her to rub it on her arm or leg or other parts of her body.

▲ Encourage her to name the part of the body as she rubs it.

Where Is Jamil's Toe?
•••••••••••••••••••••••••••

Teaches about parts of the body

▲ As you give your child a bath, take a washcloth and cover a part of his body as you sing the following song to the tune of "The Farmer in the Dell":

> *Where is (child's name) toe?*
> *Oh, where is (child's name) toe?*
> *Hi, ho, the derry-o*
> *Where is (child's name) toe?*

▲ Follow this rhyme by taking off the washcloth and wiggling the toe.

▲ Sing the song again and change the words to "Here is (child's name) toe."

▲ Continue doing this with different parts of the body.

Wash Your Knee

Teaches about parts of the body

▲ Give your child a washcloth.
▲ Ask him to wash certain parts of his body that you name.
▲ Ask him to wash his knee.
▲ Help him if he is not sure where his knee is.
▲ When your child is ready, name another part of the body.
▲ When your child easily identifies a part of his body, say two parts at a time, for example "Wash your ankles and toes."
▲ This game also develops eye-hand coordination.

Playing in the Tub

Encourages water experiments

▲ Gather together all kinds of unbreakable things to take to the bathtub and let your child experiment with them.
▲ Find things for pouring, floating, sinking, sprinkling, spraying, bubbling, squeezing and blowing.
▲ Suggestions include cups, Ping-Pong balls, empty spray bottles and sponges.

Book
Games

An Original Book

Encourages imagination

- ▲ Together with your child, select pictures from magazines.
- ▲ Cut out the pictures and paste them individually on a piece of cardboard. Each piece of cardboard should be the same size.
- ▲ Punch holes in the cardboard and attach them together by putting yarn through the holes and tying it.
- ▲ Now you have a special book that you created with your child.
- ▲ Look at the pictures and make up a story to go with the pictures.

Wheels So Round

• •

Teaches about forward and backward

▲ This is a good game to play after reading books about trains.

▲ Say the following poem and do the actions:

> Choo-choo train with wheels so round
>   (make a circle with arms)
> Chug-a-chug-a-chug up to town. (make a "chug-chug"
>   sound and walk in a forward motion)
> Chug-chug-a-chug right back down. (walk backward)
> Forward chugging, (walk forward)
> Backward chugging, (walk backward)
> Choo-choo train with wheels so round.
>   (make a circle with arms)

▲ Encourage your child to do the actions with you.

I'm a Little Rooster

• •

Encourages language skills

▲ After looking at pictures or reading a book with roosters in it, say the following poem:

> I'm a little rooster singing "Cock-a-doodle-doo."
> Watch me strut around the yard "How do you do."
>   (put hands on hips and swing shoulders as you strut)
> I can flap my wings. (flap elbows)
> I can stretch my crown. (stretch neck)
> I can "Cock-a-doodle-do" all over the town.

Let's Read a Book
● ●

Improves language skills

▲ Reading books with your child is a joyous experience.

▲ As you read a book ask your child to identify what she sees—the animals, the shapes, the colors.

▲ Young children often will sit and look at a book for a few minutes and then walk away to do something else. This doesn't mean that they are not interested. They just have a short interest span.

▲ When you get ready to read a book, present it in a positive way. For example, "Let's read a book!"

▲ The more you read to your child, the more it will improve her language skills.

Hello, Sun
● ●

Promotes language skills

▲ One of the reasons *Goodnight Moon* by Margaret Wise Brown is so popular is the book's simple sentence structure and words that young children know and understand.

▲ Make up your own version of this book by saying, "Hello" to various things in your child's room.

▲ Say, "Hello" to the bed, the table, the window, the sky.

▲ Make up other simple sentences and change the last word. Soon your child will be filling in the last word.

▲ Here are a few suggestions: "Good-bye ...," "Let's go to the ...." or "I can...."

Peekaboo Book

Teaches about object permanence

▲ This game requires preparation before you play it.
▲ From magazines choose four or five pictures familiar to your child.
▲ Put each picture on a separate piece of cardboard. You can paste, glue or tape it.
▲ Take a piece of lightweight paper and place it over the picture and staple down one side.
▲ Take the pictures and attach them together with binder rings or staples or yarn, making the pictures into a book.
▲ When your child turns to each page and lifts up the paper, she will see the magazine picture.
▲ Each time she lifts up the flap say the name of the picture, such as, "Peekaboo horse" or "Peekaboo car."

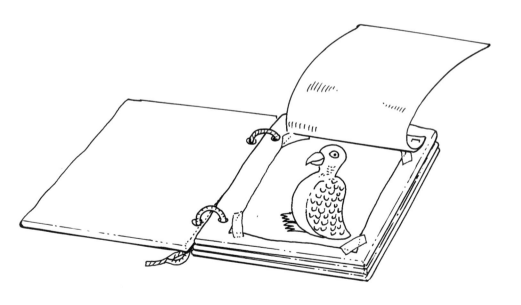

A Special Story

Teaches listening skills

▲ Children love to hear their name in a book.

▲ Pick a book that your child enjoys and substitute his name for the main character in the book.

▲ An example is the book *Where the Wild Things Are* by Maurice Sendak.

▲ Telling stories using your child's name is a wonderful way to interest your child in reading.

Where's the Bunny?

Practices observation skills

▲ This is a game that is fun to play after you have read the book *Pat the Bunny* by Dorothy Kunhardt.

▲ Hide a bunny when your child is not looking.

▲ Ask your child, "Where's the bunny?"

▲ Begin to ask questions, such as, "Is it on the chair?" or "Is it under the table?"

▲ As you ask the questions, go to that place and look for the bunny.

▲ It's a good idea to make the third question the correct place. For example, when you hide the bunny on the child's bed, the third question would be, "Is it on your bed?"

▲ When you find the bunny, shout, "Hooray, we found the bunny!"

Finding Specifics

● ●

Promotes observation skills

▲ Look at a favorite book with your child.
▲ Point to specific parts of a picture. For example, if you are looking at a picture of a cow, ask your child to point to the tail or the ears.
▲ If you are looking at a picture of a person, ask her to point to the person's feet or the person's tummy.

Pat the Bunny

● ● ● ● ● ● ● ● ● ● ● ● ● ● ● ● ● ● ● ●

Teaches thinking skills

▲ Read *Pat the Bunny* by Dorothy Kunhardt to your child.
▲ Take a toy bunny and ask your child to pat it on the ears.
▲ Then ask your child to pat the bunny different places on the bunny's body—its head, tummy, toes and tail.

Looking in Books

Develops thinking skills

▲ Select two or three books that your child knows and loves.
▲ Sit on the floor together with your child and talk about the books that you have selected.
▲ Ask your child to find a particular picture in one of the books.
▲ Help him if he isn't sure which book the picture is in.
▲ The more you play this game, the more exciting it becomes.
▲ This is also a wonderful way to develop a love for books and reading.

Act Out the Picture

Develops thinking skills

▲ Look through books or magazines for pictures of people doing a particular action. For example, throwing a ball or taking a bath.
▲ Choose a picture and show your child how to act out the picture. "Look at that girl. She's throwing a ball. Look at daddy, I can throw a ball too."
▲ Pretend to throw a ball.
▲ Ask your child if she can pretend to throw a ball.
▲ Always choose an action that your child knows how to do.

Silly Stuff

Encourages thinking skills

▲ Look at a favorite book with your child. Choose a book that has a story and pictures that the child knows.
▲ Ask her questions about the pictures that are not true.
▲ For example, if you are looking at Old MacDonald feeding the ducks, say, "Is that duck named Old MacDonald?"
▲ If you are looking at cows eating grass, say, "Is that a dog eating the grass?"

3 0 0 T H R E E M I N U T E G A M E S

Exercise
Games

Balloon Chasing

Teaches about air

▲ It's best to play this game outdoors.
▲ Blow up a balloon (don't tie the end) and explain to your child that when you let it go, all the air will go out and the balloon will fly all over.
▲ Say the following poem and chase the balloon on the third line:

Blowing, blowing up a balloon (pretend to blow)
Till it's nice and fat.
Let it go, oh, oh. (chase it around)
Now what do you think of that!

Be a Top

Develops balance

▲ If you have a top, let your child watch it spin.
▲ Pretend to be a top and show your child how to spin.
▲ You can spin standing up or on your bottom.
▲ Say, "Spin around and spin around and spin around and stop."
▲ On the word "stop" let your child stop and get his balance.

Wheelbarrow

Promotes coordination

▲ Ask your child to get down on her knees to crawl.

▲ Lift up her legs a few inches and encourage her to walk on her hands as she pretends to be a wheelbarrow.

▲ As you play the game, sing the following song to the tune of "Mulberry Bush":

> *This is the way we walk around*
> *Walk around, walk around.*
> *This is the way we walk around*
> *Walk and walk and stop!*

▲ On "stop" lower her legs gently to the ground.

Like to Skip

Practices coordination

▲ Say the following poem and do the actions:

> *I like to skip.*
> *I like to jump.*
> *I like to run around.*
> *I like to march.*
> *I like to sing.*
> *I like to laugh and SHOUT!*

Look What I Can Do!

Teaches coordination

▲ Say the following rhyme to your child:

> *I can clap, clap, clap. (clap your hands)*
> *Can you do it too? (help child clap his hands)*
> *I can jump, jump, jump. (jump up and down)*
> *Can you do it too? (help child jump)*
> *I can shake my head, no, no, no. (shake your head)*
> *I can bend my knees and sit down slooooooowly.*
> > *(fall to the ground)*

Chop Those Peanuts

Improves coordination

▲ Have your child copy you as you sit on the floor and lean back on your hands.
▲ Hold your legs straight out.
▲ Tell your child that you are going to chop peanuts for peanut butter.
▲ Pound your feet on the floor together or one at a time.
▲ As you are pounding, say, "Chop, chop, peanuts."
▲ This is a great exercise and can be followed with a snack of peanut butter on celery or apples.

Inside Kicking

●●●●●●●●●●●●●●●●●●●●●●●●●●●●●●●●

Promotes coordination

▲ This is a great active indoor game.
▲ Fill an old pillowcase with crumpled up newspaper.
▲ Tape the end closed.
▲ This makes a great kickball for your child.
▲ Say this rhyme to encourage your child to kick the ball.

> *One, two, three*
> *Kick the ball to me. (child kicks the ball)*
> *One, two*
> *I'll kick it back to you. (kick the ball back)*

Roll the Ball

●●●●●●●●●●●●●●●●●●●●●●●●●●●●●●

Develops coordination

▲ Sit on the floor facing your child. Roll a ball to her and encourage her to roll it back.
▲ Sing the following to the tune of "Row, Row, Row Your Boat" as you roll the ball:

> *Roll, roll, roll the ball*
> *Roll the ball to me.*
> *Merrily, merrily, merrily, merrily*
> *Roll the ball to me.*

▲ This is even more fun if there are others playing besides yourself. Each person can roll the ball to your child.

Jumping Town

Develops coordination

▲ Young children love to run, jump and experiment with climbing.
▲ Sing this song to the tune of "Mary Had a Little Lamb."
▲ Each time that you sing the song, change the action.

> Come with me to jumping town,
> Jumping town, jumping town.
> Come with me to jumping town
> Where you jump like this.

▲ Jump with your child.
▲ Other actions that you can do include hopping, running, marching, tiptoeing, swimming and turning.

Rolling

Enhances coordination

▲ Young children love to roll on the ground or floor.
▲ Begin with rolling from side to side, the easiest movement. As the child's ability improves, he can try doing somersaults.
▲ Try rolling on different surfaces. A carpet, the floor, the grass and in leaves are all different textures.
▲ Talk about how the different textures feel.

Slam Dunking ●

Teaches coordination

▲ This ball game is great fun and develops coordination at the same time.
▲ Get a fairly large waste paper basket.
▲ Use a ball that will fit comfortably in your child's hand.
▲ Start by having your child drop the ball into the basket.
▲ Little by little move farther away from the basket so that your child will have to throw the ball into it.

Hint: It's easier for a young child to throw underhanded.

Sally Go 'Round the Sun ●

Develops coordination

▲ This popular children's rhyme is a good way to practice moving in a circle.
▲ Hold your child's hands and face your child.
▲ As you say the rhyme, walk in a circle one way and then the other way as you say the words.

> Sally go 'round the sun.
> Sally go 'round the moon.
> Sally go 'round the chimney pot
> Every afternoon. Boom!
> (fall down with your child)

Walk All Around

●●●●●●●●●●●●●●●●●●●●●●●●●

Builds coordination

▲ Say the following poem and do the actions:

> *Walk all around boys, (girls)*
> *Walk all around.*
> *Eat peanut butter*
> *Walk all around.*

▲ Change the action but always say, "Eat peanut butter" on the third line.

> *Jump up and down boys, (girls)*
> *Jump up and down.*
> *Eat peanut butter*
> *Jump up and down.*

▲ Other suggestions include:

> *Tap on the ground....*
> *Don't make a sound....*
> *Turn 'round and 'round....*

Crawling Through the Jungle

Improves coordination

▲ Young children love this game. It is best played in a room with two or three pieces of furniture.

▲ Crawl around the room and go behind different pieces of furniture.

▲ Say the following poem as you crawl:

> *Crawling through the jungle,*
> *What do I see?*
> *I see a frog*
> *Looking at me.*

▲ Start hopping and say the same poem using the word "hopping" instead of "crawling."

> *Hopping through the jungle,*
> *What do I see?*
> *I see a bird*
> *Flying at me.*

▲ Start flying like a bird.

▲ Continue this game, changing to different animals.

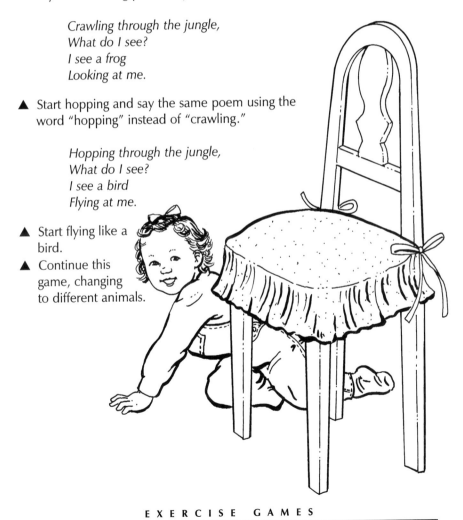

EXERCISE GAMES

Flopsy Flora

● ●

Promotes coordination

▲ Say the poem and do the actions. This is a great poem to do after exercising.

> *I have a flopsy Flora*
> *A doll that's made of rags.*
> *Her arms go flop. (flop arms like a rag doll)*
> *Her feet go plop. (flop feet like a rag doll)*
> *And her head just wigs and wags. (flop head back and forth)*

Rockin' Away

● ●

Develops coordination

▲ With a very young child rock her on her tummy. Sing a song like "Rock-a-Bye Baby" as you move her back and forth.
▲ As she gets older show her how to raise her arms and legs as she rocks.
▲ You can get on your tummy too, facing her, and hold her hands as you both rock.
▲ Sing songs as you rock and exercise at the same time.

Let's Exercise
●●●●●●●●●●●●●●●●●●●●●●●●●●●●●

Develops coordination

▲ Lie down on your back and put your child on your stomach.
▲ Hold her at the waist.
▲ Pretend to be a seesaw. When you come up, she goes down.
▲ Sing songs as you do this exercise. Some favorites are "Twinkle, Twinkle, Little Star" and "The Wheels on the Bus."
▲ This is a lot of fun and great for your stomach muscles.

Zoom, Zoom, Zoom
●●●●●●●●●●●●●●●●●●●●●●●●●●●

Develops creativity

▲ Say the following poem and do the actions:

> Zoom, zoom, zoom,
> I'm going to the moon.
> If you want to take a trip
> Climb upon my rocket ship. (pretend to climb a ladder)
> Zoom, zoom, zoom,
> I'm going to the moon.
> 10, 9, 8, 7, 6, (gradually crouch down)
> 5, 4, 3, 2, 1,
> Blast off! (jump up high and clap your hands)

Stretching

●●●●●●●●●●●●●●●●●●●●●●●

Teaches about high and low

▲ Hold your arms high in the air and stretch, stretch, stretch.
▲ Curl up on the floor just like a little mouse.
▲ Play this game with your child.

> *Stretching high, stretching high*
> *Giraffes can stretch up to the sky.*
> *Curl up like a little mouse*
> *Creepy crawl throughout the house. (crawl like a mouse)*

Carpet Squares

●●●●●●●●●●●●●●●●●●●●●●●

Practices jumping skills

▲ This game requires carpet squares that can be obtained from any carpet store.
▲ Place the squares in different patterns on the floor.
▲ Show your child how to jump from one to another.
▲ Change the patterns. Try squares, circles, triangles and zigzags.
▲ This is a wonderful game to relieve tension late in the afternoon.

Airport
● ●

Develops listening skills

▲ Designate a place in the room (or outside) to be the "airport." A favorite chair is a good place.

▲ Hold your child's hand and run in a circle. Say, "Let's land the plane at the airport."

▲ Run with your child to the designated place and stop.

▲ Hop or skip (depending on the ability of the child) around the room. Say, "Let's land the plane at the airport," then run to the designated place.

▲ Continue doing different movements and always end the activity by saying, "Let's land the plane at the airport."

▲ After you have played the game several times, whenever you say to your child, "Let's land the plane at the airport," he will most likely run to the designated place and stop.

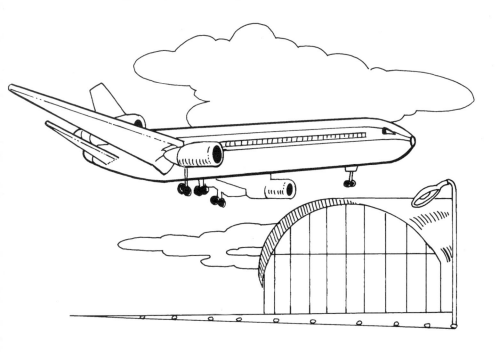

EXERCISE GAMES

Sit Down, Jump Up

Improves listening skills

▲ Sing the following song to the tune of "Are you Sleeping?"
▲ As you sing the words, do the actions.

> *Sit down, sit down,*
> *Sit down, sit down.*
> *Jump right up,*
> *Jump right up.*
> *Run, run, run, run,*
> *Run, run.*
> *Walk, walk, walk, walk,*
> *Walk, walk.*
> *Sit back down,*
> *Sit back down.*

▲ Do this slowly, then gradually faster and faster.

Cows in the Meadow

Encourages listening skills

▲ Say the following poem and do the actions:

> *Cows in the meadow*
> *Take a little nap. (lay on floor and pretend to be napping)*
> *Thunder, (stamp on the floor and make noise)*
> *Lightening, (clap hands together)*
> *Jump up and clap. (child jumps up and claps his hands)*

Roll the Ball to Daddy
●●●●●●●●●●●●●●●●●●●●●●●●●

Improves listening skills

▲ Sit on the floor facing your child.

▲ Roll a medium-size ball to her and encourage her to roll it back to you.

▲ Ask her to roll the ball to different objects in the room.

▲ Roll the ball to the chair, the table, the door.

▲ This is great fun for your child.

Jumping the Numbers
●●●●●●●●●●●●●●●●●●●●●●●●●●

Teaches about numbers

▲ Draw large numbers on pieces of cardboard or purchase large plastic numbers at a toy store or school supply store.

▲ Place the numbers on the floor. Start with three and eventually work up to the number five. (With older children use ten.)

▲ Sing the following song to the first two lines of "Twinkle, Twinkle, Little Star":

> *Can you jump on number one?*
> *Can you jump on number two?*
> *Can you jump on number two?*
> *Number two, number two.*

▲ Help your child go to the correct number and praise him each time.

Building Muscles
●●●●●●●●●●●●●●●●●●●●●●●●●●●

Develops strength

▲ Take toys of different sizes and ask your child to pick them up and hold them over her head.

▲ Start with something small. Pick something up at the same time.

▲ As the toys get heavier, show her how to use both hands.

▲ Playing this game a couple times a week will strengthen your child's muscles.

Point, Flex
●●●●●●●●●●●●●●●●●●●●●●●●●●●

Develops strength

▲ Good health is important and many exercises can be done to develop a child's muscles.

▲ Sit on a chair and stick your legs straight out in front of you.

▲ Show your child how to point his toe and then flex his foot.

▲ Sing "Point, flex, point, flex" as you do it. Singing a melody to the words makes it more fun.

▲ Another good exercise is to stand with your legs shoulder length apart and toes pointed outward. Bend your knees and lower your body and then come back up.

▲ Sing "Bend, straighten, bend, straighten" to this exercise.

Imagination Games

My First Drum
●●●●●●●●●●●●●●●●●●●●●●●●●

Encourages coordination

▲ Young children love to play with pots and pans.
▲ Give your child an aluminum or stainless steel pot and a wooden spoon.
▲ Show him how to make a drum sound by turning the pot over and banging it.
▲ Sing familiar songs as you bang away.
▲ If the noise is too much for you, put masking tape on the end of the spoon to soften the sound.

Ten Little Meatballs
●●●●●●●●●●●●●●●●●●●●●●●●●

Develops counting skills

▲ Although the words to "Ten Little Indians" are objectionable, you can use just the tune to sing songs to practice counting skills.
▲ Change the words and make up the last line to go with the subject that you have chosen.
▲ For example:

> One little, two little, three little meatballs,
> Four little, five little, six little meatballs,
> Seven little, eight little, nine little
>   meatballs,
> Ten little meatballs in spaghetti.

▲ Other suggestions include monkeys in a tree, butterflies in the sky, pumpkins in a pie.

Pumpkins

●●●●●●●●●●●●●●●●●●●●●●●●●●●

Teaches about family members

▲ Hold up one finger at a time as you say the following poem:

> *One little pumpkin sitting by the door,*
> *Mother bought another one at the grocery store.*

▲ Repeat for 2, 3, 4 and 5 pumpkins, changing the name of the person who went to the store.

> *Daddy bought another one....*
> *Sister bought another one....*
> *Brother bought another one....*

▲ End the poem with the following:

> *Five little pumpkins sitting by the door,*
> *Mother said, "That's enough, we don't need anymore!"*

Choo-Choo Train

●●●●●●●●●●●●●●●●●●●●●●●●●●

Promotes fun

▲ Hold your child's waist as you pretend to be a train.

> *Choo-choo train, choo-choo train*
> *Puffing down the track.*
> *Now we're going forward. (move forward)*
> *Now we're going backward. (move backward)*
> *Now the bell is ringing. (pull a pretend bell)*
> *Now the whistle blows. (make a "toot, toot" sound)*
> *We can make a lot of noise*
> *Everywhere we go.*

▲ Add more people and then it's even more fun.

Mommy and Child

● ●

Enhances imagination

▲ Your child is always imitating everything that you do.
▲ Try switching roles and pretend to be a child and see how your child responds.
▲ Say words that your child says and she will probably respond the way that you do.
▲ For example, say the word, "Milk." Then pretend to drink from a glass.
▲ Say the word, "More" and see if she pretends to give you more milk.
▲ The more dramatic you make this game, the more fun it is for both you and your child.

Pretending

● ●

Develops imagination

▲ Talk with your child about things that fly.
▲ Observe the birds in the sky.
▲ Where do the birds live? Go outside and try to find a bird nest.
▲ Pretend to be a bird. Fly through the sky and land in your nest.
▲ Say the following poem as you pretend to be a bird:

> *I'm a little robin flying in the sky.*
> *When I see another bird I "Tweet" as he goes passing by.*
> *Now I'm getting tired, (fly slowly)*
> *I think I better rest.*
> *Oh, it feels so good to be home in my nest.*
>
> *Jackie Silberg*

Puppets

● ●

Encourages language skills

▲ Put your hand in a sock and ask your child to do the same.
▲ Manipulate your hand to look like a mouth that is talking.
▲ Sing songs, ask questions, be silly and encourage your child to do the same.
▲ At another time, decorate the sock to look like a person or an animal.

Going Shopping

● ●

Improves language skills

▲ Before you go to the supermarket with your child, talk about what you will buy there.
▲ Say the names of the foods that she knows, such as milk, apple, orange, juice.
▲ When you get to the market, as you buy the items that you discussed, say the name of each one and talk about it.

Driving Down the Highway

• •

Builds language skills

▲ Get on the floor with your child.

▲ Have several toy cars to play with.

▲ Move the toy car around as you sing the following song to the tune of "She'll be Comin' 'Round the Mountain":

> *We are driving down the highway, here we come.*
> *We are driving down the highway, here we come.*
> *We are driving down the highway,*
> *We are driving down the highway,*
> *We are driving down the highway, here we come.*

▲ Continue singing the song and adding new verses. Here are a few ideas.

> *We are driving under the table....*
> *We are driving very fast....*
> *We are driving very slowly....*
> *We are coming to a stop*
> *sign....*

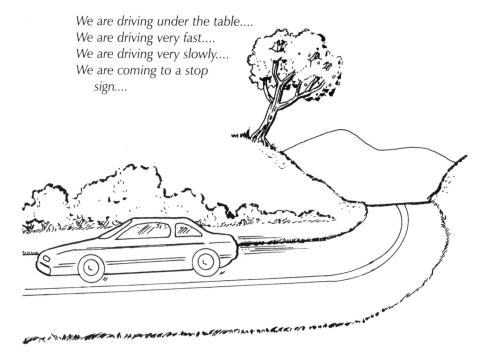

3 0 0 THREE MINUTE GAMES

Birthday Cake

● ●

Practices language skills

▲ Everyone loves birthdays. Why not pretend to make a birthday cake with your child?

▲ Say the poem and do the actions.

> Let's make a birthday cake.
> Let's make a birthday cake.
> Stir it up and stir it up. (do a stirring action)
> Put it in to bake. (open the oven door and put cake in)
>
> Open up the oven (open the oven)
> And take out the cake. (hold cake)
> Mmmm, smells so good.
> I love birthday cake.

▲ Now it's time to sing "Happy Birthday." After you sing, pretend to cut the cake and eat it.

Birthday

● ●

Teaches about large and small

▲ Say the following poem and do the actions:

> Every day when we eat dinner
> Our table is very small.
>   (make a small circle using both hands)
> There is room for my family and me
> That is all.
> But when my birthday comes,
> You won't believe your eyes.
> All my friends and relatives come
> And the table is this size. (make a great big table with both hands)

Dress Up

● ●

Teaches about parts of the body

▲ Dressing up in different clothes is a favorite game for young children.

▲ As you play dress up with your child, talk about what part of the body each piece of clothing covers.

▲ Shoes go on your feet and hats go on your head.

▲ Try changing places and put the hat on your feet and the shoe on your head.

▲ If you are putting on a shirt, discuss each part of the body as the shirt goes on. Over your head, put one arm in and then the other arm in the sleeve.

▲ You'll be amazed at how much children will learn from this game.

Ticket to Ride

● ●

Improves thinking skills

▲ Cut out ticket-size papers of different colors. The paper should be fairly sturdy. Construction paper works well.

▲ Ask your child if he would like to ride on a cow.

▲ Ask him to give you a blue ticket.

▲ When he gives you the blue ticket (help him if he doesn't know the names of colors), put him on your lap and bounce him up and down.

▲ As you are bouncing, say, "Moo, moo."

▲ Continue the game by asking for a different color ticket and using a different animal sound. With very young children use one or two colors of paper, with older children add more colors and more animals.

▲ Soon your child will tell you what animal he wants to ride on.

▲ Encourage your child to play this game with his stuffed animals.

Making Houses

● ●

Teaches thinking skills

▲ Wash out a small milk carton, the kind that is shaped like a house.
▲ Give your child stickers and let her put windows, doors and other decorations on the house.
▲ Go outside and look at your own house or apartment. Talk about the door, the windows, the chimney.
▲ This is the kind of activity that your child will love doing over and over.

Short Sentences
●●●●●●●●●●●●●●●●●●●●●●●●●●●●●

Promotes thinking skills

▲ Your child is learning to interpret language as well as saying words. If you speak in short sentences, it will help him sort out the world more easily.

▲ When you speak in short sentences or ask a short question, you are helping your child develop language and interpretative skills.

▲ Suggestions include:

> *Where is your nose?*
> *Would you please bring Daddy a car?*
> *How old are you?*
> *Please give Mommy a kiss.*
> *Where is your teddy bear?*

Making Pancakes
●●●●●●●●●●●●●●●●●●●●●●●●●●●●●

Encourages thinking skills

▲ Make pancakes one day and as you prepare them, talk about each step that you take.

▲ Get out the ingredients and mix everything together.

▲ Fry the pancake and turn it over.

▲ Eat the pancake.

▲ Say this poem with your child.

> *Mix a pancake, stir a pancake*
> *Pop it in the pan.*
> *Fry a pancake, toss a pancake*
> *Catch it if you can!*

Music
Games

Twinkle, Twinkle Little Star · Skip to My Lou · The Farmer in the Dell

Listening for Sounds
●●●●●●●●●●●●●●●●●●●●●●●●●

Develops an awareness of sound

▲ Help your child become aware of the sounds around him.

▲ Listen to the clock and try to copy the sound.

▲ Go around the room or from room to room and listen for sounds.

▲ You can also create sounds such as opening and closing a door, opening and closing a window, tapping two wooden blocks together, filling a glass with water or drawing with a crayon on paper.

▲ With older children, make a sound and see if your child can identify it. Then ask him to make a sound for you to guess.

Toy Sounds
●●●●●●●●●●●●●●●●●●●●●●●●●

Encourages an awareness of sound

▲ Think about the toys that your child enjoys. With your child, make up sounds that the toys could make.

✓ Trains—choo-choo; chug-chug.

✓ Cars—broom, broom; honk, honk.

✓ Stuffed animals and dolls—make up voices.

✓ Blocks—large pieces talk in a deep voice and smaller pieces talk in a high voice; the taller the tower, the higher the voice.

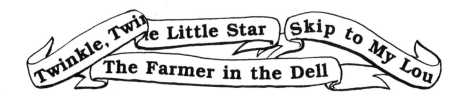

Bumpin' Along

● ●

Encourages bonding

▲ Sit on the floor with your child on your lap.

▲ Say the following as you bounce your child on your lap:

> *Bumpin' along in my little red wagon*
> *Bumpin' along in my little red wagon*
> *Bumpin' along in my little red wagon*
> *Look out, here comes a bump!*
> > *(swing your child over to one side)*

▲ Make up other verses to continue the story, such as

> *Oh, oh, the wheel is broken....*
> *I'm gonna get my hammer and*
> > *fix it....*

MUSIC GAMES

Twinkle, Twinkle Little Star · Skip to My Lou · The Farmer in the Dell

Pop Goes the Weasel

Practices coordination

▲ Sit on the floor facing your child.
▲ Each person bends her knees out and put the soles of her feet together.
▲ Hold your ankles and bury your face in your lap.
▲ Sing "Pop Goes the Weasel" and on the word "pop" lift your body up.

> *All around the cobbler's bench*
> *The monkey chased the weasel.*
> *The monkey laughed to see such sport*
> *Pop goes the weasel!*

Shake Your Fingers

Builds coordination

▲ Sing the following song to the tune of "London Bridge":

> *Shake your fingers all about, all about, all about.*
> *Shake your fingers all about,*
> *All about the town.*
>
> *Wave your fingers all about....*
> *Wiggle your fingers all about....*
> *Clap your hands all about....*
> *Throw some kisses all about....*

Twinkle, Twinkle Little Star   Skip to My Lou
The Farmer in the Dell

Singing Fun

Enhances coordination

▲ With your child pick a favorite song and sing it with your child.
▲ Sing it again and move your shoulders as you sing.
▲ Keep repeating the same song, doing a different body movement as you sing.
▲ Here are a few suggestions: tap your foot, move your elbow, shake your head, swivel your hips and shake your hand.

Walking in a Line

Develops coordination

▲ Draw a line on paper.
▲ Take a small toy and pretend to make it walk on the line you have drawn.
▲ Let your child try to make the toy walk on the line.
▲ Make a line with masking tape on the floor. Holding your child's hand, walk along the line. Sing the following song to the tune of "London Bridge":

We are walking on the line, on the line, on the line.
We are walking on the line.
Let's do it again.

We are jumping on the line....
We are crawling on the line....
We are marching on the line....

MUSIC GAMES

Dancing With Scarves
● ●

Encourages creativity

▲ Scarves make wonderful props to develop a sense of rhythm and creative expression.

▲ There are many things that you can do with a scarf.

> *Throw it in the air and watch it fall.*
> *Swish it through the air.*
> *Hold it high and run with it. As you run let it twist and bend.*

▲ Play recorded music and dance with scarves.

Heigh Ho
● ●

Teaches about daily activities

▲ Sing the following to the tune of "Heigh Ho, Heigh Ho, It's Off to Work We Go."

> *Heigh ho, heigh ho, it's off to work we go.*
> *We'll play with toys and make some noise,*
> *Heigh ho, heigh ho, heigh ho.*
> *Heigh ho, heigh ho, it's off to work we go.*
> *We'll have a day of fun and play,*
> *Heigh ho, heigh ho.*
>
> *Heigh ho, heigh ho, it's off to bed we go.*
> *We'll brush our teeth and wash our face,*
> *Heigh ho, heigh ho, heigh ho.*
> *Heigh ho, heigh ho, it's off to bed we go.*
> *We'll kiss goodnight and close eyes tight,*
> *Heigh ho, heigh ho.*

Here We Go 'Round the Mulberry Bush
●●●●●●●●●●●●●●●●●●●●●●●●●●●●●●●

Teaches about fast and slow

▲ Sing the song "Here We Go 'Round the Mulberry Bush" as you walk around in a circle.

> Here we go 'round the mulberry bush, the mulberry bush,
>   the mulberry bush.
> Here we go 'round the mulberry bush
> On a cold and frosty morning.

▲ Sing the song slowly as you walk slowly.
▲ Sing the song fast as you walk quickly.

Musical Feet
●●●●●●●●●●●●●●●●●●●●●●●●●●●●●●

Teaches about fast and slow

▲ If you have a drum, use it to play this game.
▲ If you do not have a drum, use a wooden spoon on a table top.
▲ Play a slow, steady beat and ask your child to dance to the rhythm. You may need to demonstrate.
▲ Play a fast beat and ask him to dance to the rhythm.
▲ Don't expect your child to move to the rhythm at a young age. The important thing is for him to understand the difference between fast and slow.
▲ Singing as you beat the drum adds an additional element to this game.

Hokey Pokey

• •

Teaches fun

▲ This is a bouncing song that you and your young child will enjoy together.

▲ Sit your child on your lap and bounce her up and down as you say the following rhyme:

> *Hokey pokey, penny a lump*
> *Up and down, hump, bump.*
> *If you jump you're sure to fall*
> *Hokey pokey, that is all.*

▲ On the word "all" separate your knees and let the child fall through your lap.

Opera Sounds

• •

Teaches about high and low sounds

▲ Sing about anything. When you put something away, sing, "I am putting the blocks in the basket."

▲ When you are getting your child ready for bed, sing, "We are putting on our pajamas."

▲ No matter what you are singing, you can sing it in a high voice and then in a low voice.

▲ This helps your child learn to modulate his voice.

Old MacDonald

●●●●●●●●●●●●●●●●●●●●●●●●●●●●●●

Develops language skills

▲ Young children love to sing "Old MacDonald." The animal sounds are fun but I think they really love the "E-I-E-I-O" sounds.
▲ Exploring language with different sounds is valuable and also fun.
▲ Instead of singing "E-I-E-I-O," put a consonant in front of the vowels and try singing it that way. For example, "De Di De Di Do," "Me Mi Me Mi Mo."
▲ This game is a subtle way to teach beginning sounds.

Cows in the Pasture

●●●●●●●●●●●●●●●●●●●●●●●●●●●●

Enhances language skills

▲ The song "Skip to My Lou" is wonderful for singing about barnyard animals.
▲ Ask your child what animal she would like to sing about. If necessary, suggest a cow, a horse or maybe a pig.
▲ To the tune of "Skip to My Lou" you can sing:

> *Cows in the pasture, moo, moo, moo*
> *Cows in the pasture, moo, moo, moo*
> *Cows in the pasture, moo, moo, moo*
> *Skip to my Lou my darling.*
>
> *Pigs in the pigsty, oink, oink, oink....*
> *Horse in the barnyard, neigh, neigh, neigh....*

▲ Sing about animals that your child knows.

MUSIC GAMES

Let's Make a Salad
• •

Develops language skills

▲ Make a salad and sing about each ingredient as you put it in the salad.
▲ Sing the following song to the tune of "Here We Go 'Round the Mulberry Bush":

> *This is the way we tear the lettuce,*
> *Tear the lettuce, tear the lettuce.*
> *This is the way we tear the lettuce,*
> *To make our healthy salad.*
>
> *This is the way we cut the tomato....*
> *This is the way we slice the mushrooms....*
> *This is the way we chop the peppers....*

Growing Up
• •

Teaches listening skills

▲ Pretend to be a little seed just planted in the ground.
▲ Water the little seed.
▲ Let the sun shine on the little seed.
▲ Sing the scale and pretend to grow as the music goes up.
▲ Singing the scale means singing, "Do, re, mi, fa, sol, la, ti, do," just like in the song, "Doe a deer, a female deer." from the *"Sound of Music."*
▲ When you come to the last note in the scale, say, "Look, now I'm a beautiful flower!"

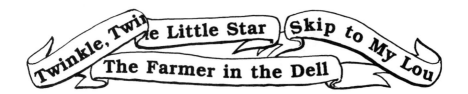

Megaphone
• •

Practices listening skills

▲ The human voice sounds different when it comes through a megaphone.

▲ Make a megaphone by cutting off the bottom of a large plastic bottle. Tape over any sharp ends.

▲ Talk into the megaphone so your child can hear your voice.

▲ Give the megaphone to your child and let him talk and sing into the megaphone.

▲ During the day, make announcements into the megaphone. "Now it's time for dinner." "Let's pick up the toys."

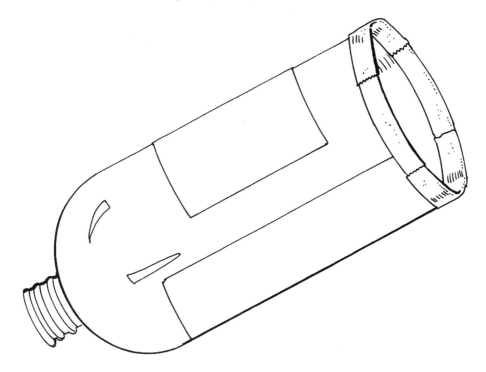

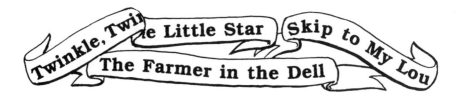

Twinkle, Twinkle Little Star — **Skip to My Lou** — **The Farmer in the Dell**

Listen to Me Sing
●●●●●●●●●●●●●●●●●●●●●●●●●

Enhances listening skills

▲ Using a tape recorder, sing songs with your child.

▲ Name the song first and then sing it. Even if your child only sings one or two words of the song, he will love listening to the tape.

▲ Announce each song before you sing it with your child.

▲ Listening to this tape of familiar songs will entertain your child at other times, such as when riding in the car.

Dance and Stop
●●●●●●●●●●●●●●●●●●●●●●●●

Teaches listening skills

▲ Hold your young child in your arms and dance around the room as you sing a familiar song.

▲ Stop singing and stop dancing. Then start singing again and start dancing.

▲ If there is another person in the room, ask him to play taped music and start and stop the music.

▲ If you stop the song at the end of each line, you are helping your child begin to understand phrasing.

Twinkle, Twinkle Little Star · Skip to My Lou · The Farmer in the Dell

Listen to the Voice
● ●

Encourages listening skills

▲ When you speak you hear your voice in one way. If you put your hands over your ears as you speak, you will hear your voice differently.
▲ This game is excellent for helping your child develop listening skills.
▲ Sing a familiar song with your child.
▲ Then sing the song again while you hold your hands over your ears.
▲ Sing the song again while pressing your fingers against your nose.

Loud Sounds
● ●

Teaches about loud and soft

▲ Take a wooden spoon and hit it against an aluminum or stainless steel pan.
▲ Take the same spoon and hit it against another spoon.
▲ As you are making the sounds, say the following rhyme:

Bang, bang, bang (in a loud voice)
Loud sounds, loud sounds
Bang, bang, bang (in a soft voice)
Soft sounds, soft sounds.

▲ Experiment with hitting the spoon on different objects to see if they make a loud sound or a soft sound.

Big and Little Noises

● ●

Teaches about loud and soft

▲ Clap your hands loudly and tell your child that this is a big noise.
▲ Ask your child to clap with you and make a big noise.
▲ Clap your hands softly and tell your child this is a little noise.
▲ Ask your child to clap with you and make a little noise.
▲ Make big and little animal sounds, such as a lion's roar and a kitty's meow.
▲ If possible, follow this game by looking at a picture book of animals and talking about the sounds that they make.

Clap, Clap

● ●

Teaches about numbers

▲ Take your child's hands in yours and clap them two times. As you clap, say the words, "One, two."
▲ Now clap your hands and say, "One, two."
▲ Each time you finish saying the words, "One, two," shout, "Hooray!"
▲ Now take turns. First your child claps with you holding her hands. "One, two, hooray!"
▲ Next you do the clapping alone.
▲ Keep playing the game and soon your child will want to do it by herself.
▲ With older children, count to five or even ten.

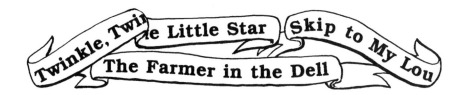

Twinkle, Twinkle Little Star Skip to My Lou
The Farmer in the Dell

Now It's Time

Teaches about parts of the body

▲ Sit on the floor with your child and sing the following song to the tune of "London Bridge" and do the actions:

Now it's time to touch our nose
Touch our nose, touch our nose.
Now it's time to touch our nose
My fair (child's name).

Now it's time to blink our eyes....
Now it's time to touch our toes....
Now it's time to shake our feet....
Now it's time to stand up tall....
Now it's time to sit back down....

Jelly in the Bowl

•••••••••••••••••••••••••••••••

Promotes rhythm skills

▲ Say the following poem and do the actions:
▲ Start saying the poem slowly. Each time that you repeat the poem, say it faster and faster.

> *Jelly in the bowl (march to the rhythm of the words)*
> *Jelly in the bowl*
> *Wibble, wobble, wibble, wobble (shake all over)*
> *Jelly in the bowl. (march again)*

▲ Each time you say the poem faster, it gets sillier to do. Your child will love it.

Cardboard Music

•••••••••••••••••••••••••••••••

Encourages rhythm skills

▲ Give your child a cardboard toilet paper tube.
▲ Show her how to make a musical sound by singing into the tube.
▲ If you sing, "Toot, toot, toot," you will make an interesting sound.
▲ Try "toot tooting" familiar songs.
▲ Popular ones include "Happy Birthday" and "Twinkle, Twinkle, Little Star."
▲ Playing this game is a forerunner to playing a kazoo and later a wind instrument.

Twinkle, Twinkle Little Star Skip to My Lou
The Farmer in the Dell

Where, Oh, Where
● ●

Develops a sense of humor

▲ Cover your eyes with your hands and sing the following song to the tune of "Paw Paw Patch":

> *Where, oh, where is (child's name)?*
> *Where, oh, where is (child's name)?*
> *Where, oh, where is (child's name)?*
> *One, two, three and Boo!*
>> *(take your hands away from your eyes)*

▲ Your child will love the element of surprise when you say, "Boo" and will anticipate it each time.
▲ As your child grows older, you can ask him to hide and reveal his hiding place on the word "boo."

It's Party Time
● ●

Enhances thinking skills

▲ Sing the following song to the tune of "The Farmer in the Dell":

> *It's birthday party time.*
> *It's birthday party time.*
> *Hi ho the derry-o,*
> *It's birthday party time.*

▲ Ask what happens at a birthday party? Let your child tell you and then sing about it in the song.
▲ With younger children you may want to give suggestions, such as

> *It's time to eat the cake....*
> *It's time to blow the candles....*
> *Let's open up the presents....*

MUSIC GAMES

Twinkle, Twinkle Little Star Skip to My Lou
The Farmer in the Dell

Rock-a My Soul

● ●

Develops trust

▲ Sing this song as you hold your child in your lap:

Rock-a my soul in the bosom of Abraham.
Rock-a my soul in the bosom of Abraham.
Rock-a my soul in the bosom of Abraham.
Oh, rock-a my soul. (rock your child back and forth)

So, high, you can't get over it.
So low, you can't get under it.
So wide, you can't get around it, (give child a big hug)
Oh, rock a my soul. (continue rocking)

▲ You will find that your child will ask to do this over and over.

Outside Games

Feeding the Birds
●●●●●●●●●●●●●●●●●●●●●●●●●●●●

Teaches about caring for others

▲ Pretend to be a bird with your child. Fly around with your arms spread out saying, "Tweet, tweet."

▲ You can do this inside or outside. If you are outside, look around for birds. Ask your child, "What do the birds eat?"

▲ Observe the birds looking for food.

▲ Sprinkle bird seed outside and watch the birds eat it.

Looking for Green
●●●●●●●●●●●●●●●●●●●●●●●●●●●

Teaches about colors

▲ Take a single colored piece of cloth and use it to make a bracelet for your child. (You can also tie a strip of cloth around her wrist.)

▲ Go outside for a walk and look for the same color as the bracelet in the grass, on the trees, anywhere outside.

▲ Green is a good color to use because you will find a lot of green things outside.

▲ When you come back from your walk, eat some celery or broccoli.

▲ Try this another day with a different color.

Ring That Bell
●●●●●●●●●●●●●●●●●●●●●●●●●●●

Develops coordination

- ▲ This is a good outside game.
- ▲ Hang a bell from a low branch on a tree. Small wind chimes work well. The bells need to be low enough so that your child can throw something at them and make them ring.
- ▲ Give your child beanbags (or soft balls) and show him how to throw the beanbags (or soft balls) at the bell.
- ▲ For young children, throwing underhanded is the easiest.

Splish Splash
●●●●●●●●●●●●●●●●●●●●●●●●●●

Develops coordination

- ▲ This outdoor game is lots of fun.
- ▲ Fill a bucket with water.
- ▲ Give your child a medium-size ball and let him throw the ball into the bucket.
- ▲ Each time the ball lands in the bucket say, "Splish, splash."
- ▲ Wear clothes that are suitable for getting wet.

Footsie Pop

Develops coordination

▲ Young children (and many adults) love to take off their shoes. This is a good barefoot game to play in the grass.

▲ Both you and your child take off your shoes.

▲ Lay down on the ground with your feet facing one another.

▲ Say the following, "One, two, three and footsie pop!"

▲ On the words "footsie pop," lift your legs in the air and touch the soles of your child's feet with the soles of your feet.

▲ Once your child gets the idea, she will absolutely love this game.

▲ An enjoyable variation is to let your child put a sticker on the bottom of each foot. Change the words from "footsie pop" to "footsie dog" or whatever is on the sticker.

Chalk Games
● ●

Develops creativity

▲ Colored chalk is a great medium for young children. It is easy to manipulate and children enjoy their artistic efforts.
▲ Find a place outside where you have the freedom to experiment with chalk.
▲ Take the chalk and draw lines as you say the words, "Up" and "Down."
▲ Give him the chalk and let him make his lines. Talk about his drawing, the color of the lines and the shapes he makes.

Outside Driving
● ●

Enhances imagination

▲ Bring toy cars and trucks outside.
▲ Take outside chalk and draw pretend roads on the sidewalk.
▲ Show your child how to move her toy car along the road.
▲ Play with her and say things, such as, "Beep, beep, get out of the way please."
▲ Suggest driving somewhere, to grandma's house, to the supermarket or to visit a friend.
▲ Give your child some chalk and let her make streets and roads.

Little Squirrel

Develops language skills

▲ This is a good fingerplay to do when you are outside looking at squirrels.

▲ Point to each finger as you say the words.

> This little squirrel said, "I want to play."
> This little squirrel said, "Let's look for nuts today."
> This little squirrel said, "Nuts are good."
> This little squirrel said, "Yummy, yummy, food."
> This little squirrel climbed up the tree,
>   (climb fingers up to your shoulder)
> And cracked those nuts...one, two, three!

The Wind

Teaches language skills

▲ If you live in a cold part of the country, this game will be very meaningful.

▲ Blow gently against your hand. Ask your child if he can blow. Tell him he is blowing like the wind.

▲ Try blowing in different ways, soft, hard, with a "whooo" sound.

▲ Say the following nursery rhyme:

> The North wind doth blow
> And we shall have snow,
> And what will robin do then, poor thing!
> He'll sit in the barn
> And keep himself warm
> And tuck his head under his wing, poor thing.

▲ This is an excellent poem for children to act out.

Outdoor Bathtub
● ●

Improves language skills

▲ This is an enjoyable outside game.
▲ Fill a large container with water. Put some toys in the container.
▲ Wash the toys with your child.
▲ Name the parts of the toys as you wash them.
▲ Wash the wheels, the top, the bottom, the outside. As you wash a part, ask your child if she can wash that part too.

Growing Things
● ●

Teaches about nature

▲ Say the following nursery rhyme to your child:

> *Mistress Mary, quite contrary*
> *How does your garden grow?*
> *With silver bells and cockle shells*
> *And pretty maids all in a row.*

▲ Ask your child what she would grow in her garden. Talk about things that grow—flowers, trees, vegetables.
▲ A good follow-up activity to this rhyme is to plant seeds and watch them grow over a period of time.

O U T S I D E   G A M E S

Grasshoppers
●●●●●●●●●●●●●●●●●●●●●●●●●●●●●●

▲ Show your child how to click his tongue to make the sound of a grasshopper.
▲ Show your child how to jump like a grasshopper.
▲ Go outside and pretend to be grasshoppers.
▲ Give your child directions: "Hop to the tree," "Hop to the fence," "Hop to the flowers."
▲ While you are outside, look for other insects.

Treasures
●●●●●●●●●●●●●●●●●●●●●●●●●●●●●●

Encourages observation skills

▲ Tie a piece of masking tape around your child's wrist with the sticky side out. Tie a piece of masking tape on your wrist also.
▲ Go on a walk. As you walk along, talk about what you see—the grass, the leaves.
▲ Pick up a leaf and stick it on your masking tape bracelet.
▲ Soon your child will be picking up leaves and sticking them on your bracelet and his bracelet also.
▲ Talk about how the leaves feel and smell.

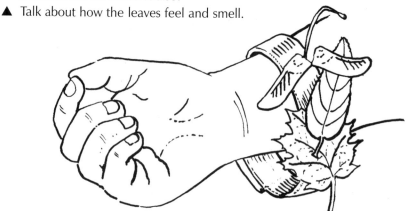

Step on a Crack

Develops observation skills

▲ Remember the saying, "Step on a crack and you'll break your mother's back. Step on a line and you'll break your mother's spine."
▲ Try a variation of that game, such as, "Step on a crack and you'll come back. Step on a line and feel just fine."
▲ Go for a walk and look for lines and cracks to step on.
▲ After you have stepped on them, try to jump over them.
▲ If you can't find lines or cracks outside, draw them with chalk.

Pick up the Trash

Teaches about picking up trash

▲ Go outside for a walk with your child. Take a large trash bag with you.
▲ Say the following poem:

> *Pick up the trash.*
> *Pick up the trash.*
> *Let's go*
> *Pick up the trash.*

▲ When you see something on the street that is trash, say, "Here's some trash. Let's put it in the bag."
Note: You may want to wear gloves when picking up trash and limit yourselves to picking up only paper trash.
▲ Your child will enjoy this game because young children love to put things in bags.
▲ This game also helps young children learn to put things in bags rather than in their mouths.

Flower Fun

• •

Promotes sensory development

▲ Gather together a bouquet of flowers. Have at least two or more different kinds of flowers in the bouquet.

▲ Smell one of the flowers and say, "Oh, that smells so nice." Give the flower to your child to smell.

▲ Take a second flower and do the same.

▲ Now take the first flower that you smelled and smell it again, but this time call it by name. "Oh, this iris smells so nice." Give the flower to your child and say, "Would you like to smell the iris?"

▲ Ask your child to give you the iris to smell.

▲ Talk about the color of the flowers, the shapes, the petals and how they feel.

Warm Weather Fun

• •

Teaches thinking skills

▲ Sit outside with your child and enjoy the moment.

▲ Select three items from the outdoors, such as a blade of grass, a small rock and a leaf.

▲ Tell your child to choose one of the three items and move it up and down your arm while your eyes are closed. Identify the item.

▲ Then ask your child to close her eyes. Pick one of the same three items and rub it up and down her arm. Encourage her to identify the item. Give clues if necessary.

▲ This game requires a lot of cognitive thinking and heightens sensory awareness.

Quiet Games

Zoom Ba
● ●

Promotes bonding

▲ Hold your young child in your arms and rock her back and forth.
▲ Say the following rhyme and do the actions:

> *Zoom ba ba, Mommy's child.*
> *Zoom ba ba, Mommy's child.*
> *Cover her up and pat her on the head.*
> *Give her a little kiss and put her to bed.*

▲ Repeat this poem using the names of other members of the family instead of Mommy.

Cobbler, Cobbler
● ●

Enhances bonding

▲ This is a good game to play before going to bed.
▲ Sit your young child on your lap.
▲ Ask him to take off his shoes. This is a favorite activity for young children.
▲ Cup your hand over his foot and say the following poem:

> *Cobbler, cobbler, mend my shoe.*
> *Get it done by half past two.*
> *My toe is peeping through. (adjust your hand so that you can see a toe)*
> *Cobbler, cobbler, mend my shoe.*

▲ Take his toe and give it a big kiss.

Cows

● ●

Encourages bonding

▲ This rhyme comes from China.

▲ Tickle each toe as you say the rhyme.

> *This little cow eats grass.*
> *This little cow eats hay.*
> *This little cow drinks water.*
> *This little cow runs away.*
> *This little cow does nothing*
> *But lie down all the day.*

▲ Pretend to go to sleep.

Let's Go to the Woods

● ●

Encourages bonding

▲ This is a good game to play before bedtime.

▲ Say the following poem and do the actions:

> *"Let's go to the woods," said this little pig.*
>   *(wiggle child's left foot)*
> *"What will we do there?" said this little pig.*
>   *(wiggle child's right foot)*
> *"Look for our mother," said this little pig.*
>   *(wiggle child's left arm)*
> *"What shall we do with mother?" said this little pig.*
>   *(wiggle child's right arm)*
> *"Kiss her all over," said this little pig.*
>   *(kiss child all over)*

Sleepy Head
●●●●●●●●●●●●●●●●●●●●●●●●●●●●

Promotes bonding

▲ Hold your child in your arms as you say the following poem:

Sleepy head, sleepy head
Now it's time to go to bed.
Now it's time to say goodnight
Close your eyes and shut them tight.

If I Had a Donkey
●●●●●●●●●●●●●●●●●●●●●●●●●●●

Improves bonding

▲ Say the following rhyme as you bounce your child on your knee:

If I had a donkey and he wouldn't go,
Do you think that I would spank him?
Oh, no, no.
I'd put him in the barn and give him some corn,
The best little donkey that ever was born.
    (give your child a hug)

Riding to Bed

Encourages bonding

▲ Slowly (very slowly) bounce your young child on your knee as you say the following rhyme:

> *Ride on Daddy's knee, dear.*
> *And see what you can see, dear.*
> *I see (child's name) eyes, dear.*
> *And I see (child's name) nose, dear.*
> *Time to go to bed, dear.*
> *Nighty, nighty, night, dear.*

▲ Repeat the rhyme. This time hold your child and say it softly.
▲ This is a perfect rhyme to say before it is time to take a nap or to go to sleep at bedtime.

Spools of Thread

Teaches about colors

▲ This game teaches about counting, colors and much more.
▲ Take a basket and fill it with many different colored spools of thread.
▲ Here are suggestions for things you and your child can do with the spools of thread when you have a few minutes.

✓ Match colors
✓ Count the spools
✓ Build a tower
✓ Make a circle with the spools and pretend it is a play yard, a circus ring or a street on which to push toy cars.

Color Fun

•••••••••••••••••••••••••••••

Teaches about colors

▲ Choose one color (red is good) and put several items of that color into a container.

▲ Ask your child to give you one of the items. Always say the name of the color when asking. For example, "Would you please give me the red mitten?"

▲ If your child gives you another item, say, "Thank you for giving me the red car. Let's look for the red mitten. Here it is."

▲ When you feel that your child can identify one color, put items of two colors in the container and help her distinguish the colors by asking for items of one color and then the other. For example, "Please give me the red ball. Thank you. Now please hand me the blue truck."

▲ This game gives a child practice in recognizing colors.

Me and You

•••••••••••••••••••••••••••••

Teaches about the concept of two

▲ Say the following poem to your child:

> *Me and you (point to self and then to child)*
> *We make two. (hold up two fingers)*
> *One, two, (point to each finger as you count it)*
> *Cock-a-doodle-doo. (flap your arms and run around in a circle)*
>
> *See my hands*
> *I have two. (hold up both hands)*
> *One, two,*
> *Cock-a-doodle-doo. (repeat as above)*
> *Jackie Silberg*

▲ Keep repeating the poem with the actions as you name the paired parts of your body, such as eyes, ears, feet, thumbs.

Sculptures

●●●●●●●●●●●●●●●●●●●●●●●●●●●●●●

Builds coordination

▲ You will need pipe cleaners for this game.
▲ Bend a pipe cleaner into a circle.
▲ Put your finger through the circle and wiggle it.
▲ Now ask your child to put his finger through the circle and wiggle it.
▲ Change the shape of the pipe cleaner.
▲ Give it to your child and encourage him to change the shape again.
▲ With older children, make specific geometric shapes, such as squares, rectangles and triangles and talk about the shapes.

Beanbag Fun

●●●●●●●●●●●●●●●●●●●●●●●●●●●●

Improves coordination

▲ Gather together two or three brightly colored pillows (solid colors, if possible).
▲ Talk about the colors of the pillows with your child.
▲ Give your child a beanbag and ask her to throw it at the pillows.
▲ You can make a game out of this by saying, "One, two, three, throw!"
▲ Once she has mastered throwing the beanbag at the pillow, ask her to throw it at the red pillow or the green pillow.
▲ This game provides practice in recognizing colors.

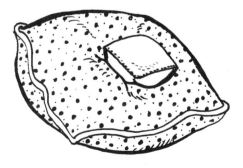

Ten Red Apples
●●●●●●●●●●●●●●●●●●●●●●●●●

Practices counting skills

▲ Say the following poem and do the actions:

> Ten red apples growing on a tree.
> *(hold arms up in the air like branches)*
> Five for you and five for me.
> *(shake one hand and then the other)*
> I will shake the tree just so, *(shake body)*
> And let the apples fall below.
> *(move fingers downward through the air)*
> One, two, three, four, five,
> *(count fingers on one hand)*
> Six, seven, eight, nine, ten.
> *(count fingers on the other hand)*

The Counting Game
●●●●●●●●●●●●●●●●●●●●●●●●

Encourages counting skills

▲ Count your fingers on one hand. Touch each finger and say the numbers out loud.
▲ Count the fingers on one of your child's hands. Touch each finger and say the numbers out loud.
▲ Repeat the same counting with toes.
▲ Say the following rhyme:

> Touch your fingers.
> Touch your toes.
> Now we'll count them.
> Ready, set, go.

▲ Count up to five. With older children use both fingers and toes to count to twenty.

One, Two, Three

Promotes fun

▲ Many young children love to be held high in the air.

▲ Hold your child in your arms. Count, "One, two" and on the word "three" raise him high into the air.

▲ You can also turn in a circle or let the child drop through your legs on "three."

▲ Soon, he will anticipate the word "three" and start laughing even before it is said.

Cotton Balls

Encourages imagination

▲ What can you do with a cotton ball? Here are a few suggestions:

✓ Squish a bunch in your hand and make a big ball.
✓ Line them up to make lines and circles.
✓ Count them.
✓ Balance them on different parts of your body—your head, your shoulder, your nose.
✓ Walk with them between your toes.

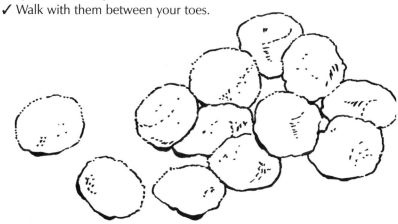

QUIET GAMES

Stamps

●●●●●●●●●●●●●●●●●●●●●●●●●●●

Develops imagination

▲ Rubber stamps are easy to obtain and young children love to use them.

▲ Give your child a large piece of paper. Tape it to the table to keep it in one place.

▲ Put out an assortment of rubber stamps (one or two for young children, more for older ones) and a stamp pad.

▲ Let her stamp all over the paper.

▲ With older children, ask them to stamp in a particular pattern or design. With young children, let them stamp in their own way.

▲ Use the paper as gift wrap.

Little Peanuts

Practices language skills

▲ Children enjoy this action rhyme.

> See the little peanuts lying in the pan.
>> (lie down curled up)
> Watch the little peanuts wiggle in your hand.
>> (wiggle around)
> Open up the peanut.
>> (stand up and stretch)
> Put it in your tummy.
>> (pretend to eat the peanut)
> Wasn't that delicious?
>> (rub tummy)
> Yummy, yummy, yummy.

Quiet Sounds

Teaches listening skills

▲ Nap and bedtime can sometimes be stressful for a young child if they are disturbed by outside noises.
▲ Help your child become familiar with the noises by calling attention to them.
▲ Birds, sirens, footsteps, airplanes are all noises that can be identified.
▲ Play a game to help him identify the sounds by asking the question, "What sound do you hear?"
▲ This game may make going to sleep much easier.

Kisses

● ●

Teaches about parts of the body

▲ Hold your child in your lap. Rock him and say the following rhyme:

> *Yellow, orange, red and blue.*
> *Here's a little kiss for you.*

▲ Kiss your index fingertip and place it on your child's nose.
▲ Say, "I put the kiss on your nose."
▲ Repeat the poem again and place the kiss on another part of your child's body, such as her knee, her eye, her shoulder, her finger. Each time tell the child where you placed the kiss.
▲ Ask your child where she would like the kiss.
▲ This game also helps develop language skills.

Two Little Dickey Birds

Enhances listening skills

▲ This is an enjoyable game to play before going to bed.
▲ Say the following poem and do the actions:

> *Two little dickey birds (hold up index fingers)*
> *Sitting on a wall.*
> *One named Peter, (wiggle one finger)*
> *One named Paul. (wiggle the other finger)*
> *Fly away, Peter. (fly finger behind back)*
> *Fly away, Paul. (fly other finger behind back)*
> *Come back, Peter. (return finger)*
> *Come back, Paul. (return other finger)*

▲ This poem is also known as "Two Little Blackbirds."
▲ A variation (to use at other times) is to let your child pretend to fly to a designated place and then return.

Buttoning

Promotes self-help skills

▲ Learning to button and unbutton is an acquired skill that takes practice. Your young child will be thrilled when he has accomplished this skill.
▲ It's easier to practice buttoning and unbuttoning with an adult's coat or sweater. Once he is successful with an adult's coat, encourage him to try his own clothes.
▲ Zippers work the same way. Start with big zippers first.

Sounds and Textures

● ●

Teaches about smooth and rough

▲ Play this game with your child watching. Then give him another piece of paper and play the game again.

▲ Take a piece of paper, rub your hand across it and say, "Smooth."

▲ Crumple the piece of paper into a ball, run your hand across it and say, "Rough."

▲ Open and close your hand on the paper ball and say, "Listen."

▲ Repeat the above steps with your child holding the piece of paper. Guide his hands as he repeats the same actions.

Storytelling Games

Baby Pictures

●●●●●●●●●●●●●●●●●●●●●●●●●●●●●●

Develops an awareness of self

▲ Look at the pictures you took of your child when he was an infant.

▲ Look at recent pictures.

▲ Say, "Look at your hands when you were a baby. Look at your eyes in this picture. Your hands and fingers can do more things now than when you were a baby." Talk about those things, for example, feed himself, undress himself.

▲ Point out different parts of the body and how they have changed.

▲ Look in the mirror and talk about the same parts of the body as you did when looking at the pictures.

A Little Boy

●●●●●●●●●●●●●●●●●●●●●●●●●●●●●

Develops creativity

▲ This is a great rhyme that is perfect for acting out with young children.

▲ First say the poem and show your child how to lie down on the pretend hay.

▲ When your child is ready for a new role say the poem again and show your child how to be the owl.

▲ Finally, when your child is ready, say the poem again and let your child be the little boy. You can be the owl.

▲ Try switching parts.

> *There was a little boy (girl) who lived in the barn.*
> *He (she) took a little nap on some hay.*
> *Mr. Owl came in and flew all around,*
> *And the little boy (girl) ran away.*

Making Faces

Teaches about emotions

▲ Show your child how to make different kinds of faces. Happy, silly, sad and angry are good ones to begin with.

▲ Tell your child that you are going to make a happy face. Ask him to copy you and make his own happy face.

▲ Continue with other kinds of faces. Always tell your child which face you are going to make and ask him to copy you.

▲ Make up a story using the different emotions that you have talked about. When you use the words, happy, silly, sad and angry, make your voice express the same emotion as your face expresses.

Peter, Peter
●●●●●●●●●●●●●●●●●●●●●●●●●●●

Encourages fun

▲ I have changed the words to this nursery rhyme to reflect a more positive attitude toward women.

> Peter, Peter Pumpkin Eater (hold child's hands and walk in a circle)
> Had a wife and loved to keep her.
> Put her in a pumpkin shell (circle your arms around child's waist)
> And there he hugged her very well. (give child a big hug)

Who Took the Cookies?
●●●●●●●●●●●●●●●●●●●●●●●●●●●

Promotes fun

▲ Start this game by telling a story. "Once upon a time was a jar full of cookies. One day, daddy went to get a cookie and they were all gone."
▲ Then, say the following poem:

> Who took the cookies from the cookie jar?
> Daddy took the cookies from the cookie jar.
> Who me? Yes, you.
> Couldn't be. Then, who?

▲ Repeat using your child's name.
▲ Keep saying the rhyme and name other members of the family, pets and people your child knows.
▲ For example, "Who took the cookies from the cookie jar? Grandma took the cookies from the cookie jar."

Mail Time

●●●●●●●●●●●●●●●●●●●●●●●●●

Enhances imagination

▲ Put junk mail in a basket or just hold it in your hand.
▲ Say, "The mail is here. Here's a letter for you."
▲ Let your child pick up the pieces of mail and look at them.
▲ Pick up a piece and pretend to read it. "Dear (child's name), I like playing blocks with you. Love, Daddy."

Pussy Cat, Pussy Cat

●●●●●●●●●●●●●●●●●●●●●●●●

Promotes imagination

▲ Your young actor can pretend to be the cat as you say this nursery rhyme.
▲ You will need a chair for your child to hide under.

> *Pussy cat, pussy cat, where have you been?*
> *I've been to London to visit the Queen.*
> *Pussy cat, pussy cat, what did you there?*
> *I frightened a little mouse under the chair.*

▲ As you say the last line, the pussy cat says, "Meow, meow" and pretends to chase a mouse.

Wee, Wee
●●●●●●●●●●●●●●●●●●●●●●●●●●●●●

Practices imagination

▲ Tell your child that you are the mommy pig and he is the baby pig.
▲ Baby pigs say, "Wee, wee."
▲ Ask your baby pig questions and tell him to answer in baby pig language.
▲ Questions to ask include:

> *Did you have a good breakfast?*
> *Answer: wee, wee*
> *Will you please show me how you run?*
> *Answer: wee, wee (as child runs)*

▲ This is a fun game for a young child who has only beginning language skills.

The Flower Story
●●●●●●●●●●●●●●●●●●●●●●●●●●●

Enhances imagination

▲ Tell the following story and act out the parts while encouraging your child to do the same:

> *I'm a little flower who is very small.*
>   *(crouch down as small as you can)*
> *I need some sun.*
>   *(put your hands over your head to symbolize the sun)*
> *I need some water. (wiggle your fingers and say, "Swish, swish, swish")*
> *Sun and water make me grow taller and taller and taller.*
>   *(slowly rise up to a standing position and then on tiptoes)*
> *Now I'm as big as can be and everyone wants to smell me (sniff).*

The Fruit Story
● ●

Develops language skills

▲ This is a good game to play after you have played the Fruit Song game in Thinking Games on page 163.
▲ Pick two or three fruits for your child to look at.
▲ One by one cut them open and talk about what's inside. Does it have seeds, a core, segments?
▲ Tell the following story using the words from your discussion about fruit:

> *Once upon a time there was an apple that came to play with Billy. "Hi, Billy, I'm glad to be here. I am kind of lonely. Could we invite another fruit over?"*
>
> *"Okay," said Billy, "I'll call a grapefruit." Billy dialed the phone and said, "Hello, grapefruit. Would you like to come over to play?"*

▲ Continue this story naming the fruits that you have looked at and the name of your child.
▲ Finish the story by saying, "All of the fruits jumped into the blender and made a fruit shake for Billy."

STORYTELLING GAMES

The Elephant Story

Develops language skills

▲ Make up a story about an elephant who was carrying a peanut to the cook to make peanut butter.
▲ Your child is the elephant and she is carrying the peanut in a spoon.
▲ As the elephant passes different objects in the house, name them.
▲ Remember that elephants walk slowly.

> *Once upon a time there was an elephant named (child's name). She had a very important job. Her job was to carry the peanuts to the cook in the kitchen. Very carefully she walked by the chair. The chair said, "Hurrah." Next she walked by the table. The table said, "Hurrah."*

▲ Continue this story until the elephant gets to the kitchen.
▲ Eating peanut butter and crackers is a good ending to the story.

Looking at Pictures

Develops language skills

▲ Look at pictures with your child. Look at pictures of family members and talk about the pictures.
▲ Give the names of the persons and tell something about them. For example, "This is Aunt Helen and she loves to sing."
▲ This is also a good activity to do with pictures of your child's playmates.
▲ This game is especially good to play when relatives live out-of-town. It gives your child a chance to learn something about them.

Raisin Stories

Improves language skills

▲ Take a small raisin box, such as one that is used for individual servings.

▲ Put a picture of an animal or something that is familiar to your child inside the box.

▲ Give the box to your child and ask him to look inside.

▲ When he gives you the picture, make up a simple story about the picture. For example, "Once upon a time there was a little dog who loved to play with (child's name). They played and played until they got so tired that they laid down and went to sleep."

▲ A story as simple as that will interest your young child.

STORYTELLING GAMES

A Family Story

Practices language skills

▲ Tell your child a story about your family and your house.

> *Once upon a time there was a wonderful little girl named (child's name). She lived in a house with her mother (mother's name) and father (father's name) and (use the names of all adults, children and pets in the family).*
> *In their kitchen was a (name the refrigerator, the stove and other appliances).*
> *(Child's name) had many friends (name friends). When she played she loved to play (name things she likes to do).*

▲ If you play this game each day for a few minutes and start the story the same way, soon your child will fill in the names of everyone and everything.

Food and More Food

Encourages language skills

▲ Talk with your child about his favorite foods and incorporate his words into a story about meals.

> *One morning Derek woke up and he had (name the foods your child likes) for breakfast. Then he played with his toys until it was time for lunch. For lunch he ate (name the foods your child likes). For dinner he ate (name other foods your child likes).*

▲ Playing this game not only develops language skills but it also shows your child that he is important to you.

Association Stories

Develops language skills

▲ Make up a story that includes a group of things that your child knows.
▲ Set the stories in familiar places like the bathtub, the car, the bedroom and the kitchen.
▲ Here is an example.

> *Once upon a time there was a little girl who just loved taking a bath. First she would take her toy duck and splash it in the water. Then she would take her toy (let the child fill in the word) and splash it in the water.*
> *When it was time to wash, first she washed her hands. Then she washed her (let child say the word).*
> *You can end with, "Then she said, bye-bye bathtub."*

Where's the Little Bird?
●●●●●●●●●●●●●●●●●●●●●●●●●●●●●●

Teaches language skills

▲ Tell your child that this is a story about a cuckoo bird.

▲ Demonstrate a cuckoo sound.

▲ Make up a story about how the little cuckoo bird flies from place to place. Each time the bird lands, he makes the cuckoo sound.

▲ Your child will begin to copy the sound each time that you make it.

> *Once a little cuckoo bird flew around and around. He flew to the door, "Cuckoo." Then he flew to the window, "Cuckoo." He saw other birds outside the window.*

▲ You can end the story with the little bird going to his nest and going to sleep saying, "Cuckoo" (slowly and quietly).

A Moving Story
●●●●●●●●●●●●●●●●●●●●●●●●●●●●

Practices listening skills

▲ Hold your child's hand and walk around the room. As you are walking, tell this story.

> *Mommy and (child's name) were walking down the street. They stopped (stop) to see a horse and said, "Hi, Mr. Horse." The horse said, "Neigh." They started walking again until they saw a cow nearby.*

▲ Continue the story starting and stopping to see different animals. Make the animal sound of each animal.

▲ Change the mode of locomotion—run, hop, tiptoe, march.

Once Upon a Time...

Hand and Foot Stories

●●●●●●●●●●●●●●●●●●●●●●●●●●●●●●●

Teaches about parts of the body

▲ Draw an outline of your child's hand and foot.

▲ Cut the outlines out and paste them on paper. You can even make them into a book by stapling the pages together. Children love to look at books about themselves.

▲ Show the hand picture to your child and explain that the picture is an outline of her hand. Ask her to put her hand on the picture.

▲ Make up a story.

> *Once upon a time Susie's (child's name) hand went walking to her nose. (Take your child's hand and walk it to her nose.) "Hello, nose," said Susie's hand. (Wave hello with the hand.)*

▲ Continue walking the hand to different parts of the body.

▲ Play the same game with your child's foot. You'll probably have to lie down on the floor to play the foot story.

Today and Yesterday

Teaches about time

▲ Tell a story about what you did yesterday, what you did today and what you will do tomorrow.

▲ This helps your child begin to understand past, present and future.

▲ For example, "Yesterday we went to grandma's house. Today we are going to the park. Tomorrow Pedro is coming to play with you."

▲ If you do this every day, your child will soon begin to understand the concept of yesterday, today and tomorrow.

▲ This is also a good beginning game for learning about sequences.

Stuck Inside Games

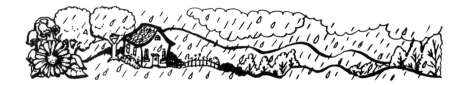

Whose Socks Are These?

Teaches about bigger and smaller

▲ Take several pairs of socks belonging to different members of the family and put them in a small basket.
▲ Take out one sock and put it on your child's foot.
▲ Ask, "Who's sock is this?"
▲ Tell him the answer.
▲ After you have tried different socks, ask him to give you sister's sock or daddy's sock.
▲ If you put the socks on the floor, you can compare the big socks to the small socks.

Feeling Ice

Teaches about cold

▲ Take an ice cube and put it into a plastic bag.
▲ Let your child hold the bag.
▲ Use the word "cold" as you encourage him to touch the bag (for a short period of time) to different parts of his body.
▲ Say, "Put the ice on your cheek. Does it feel cold?" or "Put the ice on your knee. Does it feel cold?"
▲ If the weather outside is cold, this would be a good time to make comparisons.

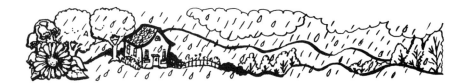

Watching Ice

Teaches about cold

▲ Now that your child has experienced the coldness of ice, you can show her how ice can change from a solid to a liquid.

▲ Put an ice cube into a bag.

▲ Ask your child to find a place in your house where there is warm air. A heating vent or a sunny window are good places.

▲ Set the ice cube on the heating vent or in the window and watch the ice begin to melt.

▲ Sing the following song to the tune of "Glow Worm":

> *Look at the ice cube, melting, melting.*
> *Look at the ice cube, melting, melting.*
> *It was cold and now it's warm so*
> *Melt little ice cube melt.*

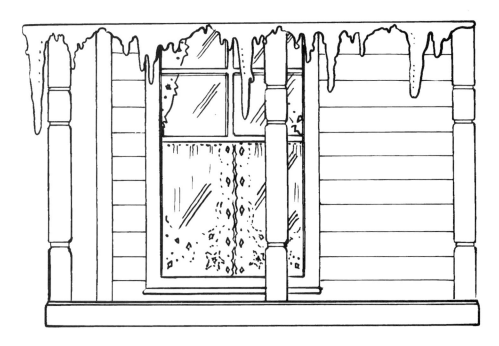

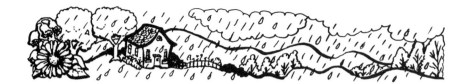

Inside Ball
●●●●●●●●●●●●●●●●●●●●●●●●●●●

Develops coordination

▲ Make a ball out of a sock. This makes a good, soft inside ball.
▲ Ask your child to throw the ball to you.
▲ Say, "One, two, three."
▲ Ask her to throw the ball on "three."
▲ With older children ask them to throw the ball at a specific target. For example, "Throw the ball on the couch."

Peeling Labels
●●●●●●●●●●●●●●●●●●●●●●●●●●

Develops coordination

▲ Take one or two sheets of labels or stickers. The larger they are, the easier it will be for your child to remove them.
▲ Help your child remove the label and put it on another sheet of paper.
▲ If there is time, your young artist can decorate the label page.
▲ This is an excellent activity for developing finger dexterity.

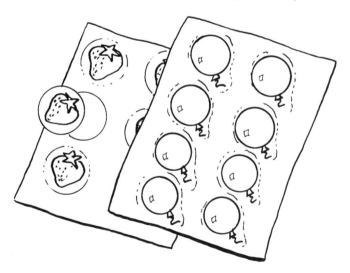

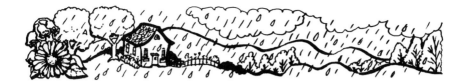

Ball Fun
● ●

Enhances coordination

▲ Take a small blanket and put it on the floor.

▲ Put a soft ball in the middle of the blanket.

▲ Show your child how to hold two corners of the blanket.

▲ You hold the other two corners.

▲ Count, "One, two, three," and gently lift up the blanket so that the ball goes into the air and falls back down on the blanket.

▲ This game can get silly, but your child will enjoy chasing the ball when it falls off the blanket.

Making Faces
● ●

Teaches coordination

▲ Talk about all the parts of the face. Point to each part and say the name aloud—nose, mouth, tongue, ears.

▲ Make a silly face like sticking out your tongue.

▲ Ask your child to copy you.

▲ Suggestions include:

 ✓ Push your nose to one side.
 ✓ Move your tongue in different directions.
 ✓ Pull your lips apart.
 ✓ Squint your eyes.

▲ Encourage your child to make his own silly faces.

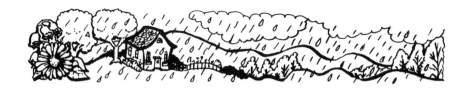

Please Help Me

Develops coordination

▲ Many kitchen jobs are perfect for your child to do while developing his finger dexterity at the same time.

▲ Whatever the job, say, "Please help me." To get your child's attention use a dramatic voice.

▲ Possible jobs include:

✓ Peeling a banana
✓ Opening up a small box of raisins
✓ Putting the silverware away
✓ Putting napkins at each plate
✓ Unwrapping a stick of margarine

One, Two

Develops counting skills

▲ Say the following poem and do the actions:

One, two, I'm gonna get you.
  (pick up your child and hold her close)
Three, four, get you more.
  (twirl in a circle while holding your child)
Five, six, let's do a trick.
  (hold your child in the air)
Seven, eight, stand up straight.
  (hold your child straight up in the air)
Nine, ten, let's do it again.
  (put your child down and start the poem again)

Number Two
• •

Teaches counting skills

▲ The number two is one of the first number concepts children begin to understand because two is everywhere.

▲ Start by counting the body parts—two eyes, two ears.

▲ If your child is two years old, he will be thrilled to hold up two fingers. If he is four, he can hold up two fingers on each hand.

▲ Count things at every opportunity that you have. The more hands-on experiences he has, the more he will understand the concept of two.

▲ When you give your child a cracker or a grape, ask him if he would like two. Put one in each hand and count them, "One, two."

▲ You will be amazed at how quickly he will begin to understand the concept of two.

Trot, Trot
• •

Encourages fun

▲ Say the following rhyme and do the actions:

Trot, trot, trot to Dover. (bounce child on your knees, facing you)
Trot, trot, trot to Dover.
Look out (child's name)
Or you might fall O-ver. (tip your child to one side)

Trot, trot, trot to Boston. (bounce child again)
Trot, trot, trot to Lynn. (hold your child's waist and neck)
Look, out (child's name)
Or you might fall in. (open your legs and let your child fall toward your ankles, holding her firmly)

Flashlight Fun
● ●

Develops imagination

▲ Show your child how a flashlight works.
▲ Shine the flashlight on her toys. Ask her about each toy as you shine the light on it.
▲ Ask her to blow out the light. When she blows, turn off the flashlight.
▲ This is a great game to play on a dark, rainy day.

Chubby Snowman
● ●

Promotes imagination

▲ It's a good (though not essential) idea to look at pictures of snowmen before doing the actions to this poem.

A chubby little snowman
Had a carrot nose. (point to your nose)
Along came a bunny, (hop around the room)
And what do you suppose?

That hungry little bunny
Was looking for some lunch.
Took that snowman's nose (pretend
*   to grab your child's nose)*
Nibble, nibble, crunch!

300 THREE MINUTE GAMES

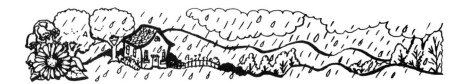

Let's Read the Mail
● ●

Promotes language skills

▲ Young children love to pretend to read.
▲ Take several envelopes of junk mail and let your child help you open the envelopes. Let her take out the letters.
▲ Talk about the pictures and read your child a pretend letter. "Dear (child's name), You have a beautiful smile. Love, Mommy."
▲ Let her "read" you a letter.
▲ The game is an enjoyable way to develop language skills.

The Magical Mystery Bag
● ●

Practices language skills

▲ Keep a canvas bag on hand to use for quick diversion.
▲ Fill it with small toys like balls, trucks and dolls.
▲ Put your hand in the bag and say, "One, two, three, what do you see?"
▲ Take an object out of the bag and let your child tell you what it is.
▲ Make up a story about the toy and when you finish the story, say to your child, "Would you please put the toy back into the magical mystery bag?"
▲ This activity can keep your child busy when you are stuck inside because of bad weather.

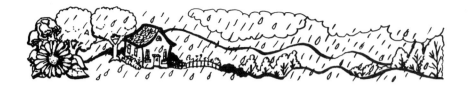

I Am

Encourages language skills

▲ This game is full of learning experiences to share with a young child.

▲ Tell your child that whatever you ask him, he will answer, "I am."

▲ If your child is not talking yet, say, "(Child's name) is."

▲ Tap your shoulder against your child's shoulder and say, "Who is tapping shoulders?"

▲ Your child answers, "I am."

▲ Take your child's hands and lift them in the air. Then ask, "Who is holding his hands in the air."

▲ Child answers, "I am."

▲ Continue asking all kinds of questions. With older children use more complex questions and let him give his own response.

Mrs. Roobie Doobie

Teaches listening skills

▲ Say the words, "Mrs. Roobie Doobie, can I come to your house?"

▲ Say the words with your child until she can say them by herself.

▲ Have your child ask you the question, "Mrs. Roobie Doobie, can I come to your house?"

▲ Suggested ways to answer the question include:

✓ You may come to my house, if you ask in a soft voice.
✓ You may come to my house, if you ask in a loud voice
✓ You may come to my house, if you ask in a whisper voice.

▲ Continue playing the game and help your child ask the questions in the different voices.

Toy Talk
• •

Develops listening skills

▲ Give your child one of her favorite toys.
▲ Pretend to be the toy talking and ask your child to put the toy in different places.
▲ For example, "(Child's name), please put me on the chair."
▲ When your child puts the toy on the chair, say, "Thank you, I like the chair."
▲ Other directions that you can give in your toy voice are to put the toy behind things, under things and in front of things.

Bouncing Ball
• •

Practices listening skills

▲ Balls can bounce up and down and roll back and forth. Show your child how to bounce a ball and roll a ball.
▲ Say the following poem and change the directions each time:

> *Ball, ball, bouncing ball,*
> *Can you bounce to the door?*
>
> *Ball, ball, rolling ball,*
> *Can you roll to the chair?*

▲ Depending on the age of your child, use words like "forward," "backward" and "sideways."

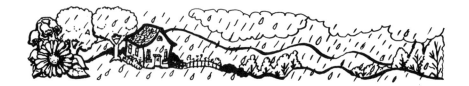

Shake It Around
● ●

Improves listening skills

▲ Shakers make wonderful toys. If you don't have any, make them. Take a margarine tub and fill it with large buttons, large paper clips, small spoons or any suitable materials. Tape it securely.

▲ Give your child directions on where to shake the shaker.

✓ Shake it high.
✓ Shake it low.
✓ Shake it to the side.
✓ Shake it behind you.
✓ Shake it in front of you.

▲ Continue playing the game by adding your own ideas.

Who Is Clapping?
● ●

Teaches listening skills

▲ Take your child's hand and clap them together. Say, "Who is clapping hands? Susie (child's name) is, Susie is."

▲ Repeat asking your child to try other actions.

✓ Who is tiptoeing?
✓ Who is jumping?
✓ Who is hopping?
✓ Who is crawling?

▲ Always say, "(child's name) is," following each action.

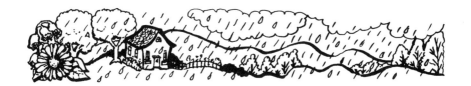

Trading Pasta
● ●

Teaches matching skills

▲ Pour two or three different shapes of dried pasta into one bowl. Use more varieties with older children.
▲ Wash hands.
▲ Pick up a piece of pasta and give it to your child.
▲ Ask your child to find a piece like yours and give it to you. Young children may not be able to match the pieces. If that's the case, just picking up the piece of pasta and giving it to you provides practice in eye-hand coordination.
▲ Continue the game, trying to match the different shapes.
▲ To extend this game, cook the pasta and enjoy it with your child.

If You're Wearing Red
● ●

Develops observation skills

▲ Pick a color that your child is wearing.
▲ Say, "If you're wearing red, jump up and down."
▲ Continue giving directions using the same color or naming another color.
▲ Pick a color that you are wearing and play the same game.

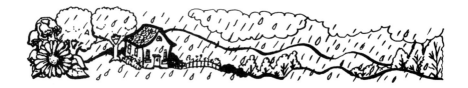

Watching the Storm
●●●●●●●●●●●●●●●●●●●●●●●●●

Practices observation skills

▲ Stormy weather can be a wonderful learning experience.

▲ Look at the clouds and talk about the dark sky and the dark clouds.

▲ Play listening games and identify the sounds of the rain, lightning and thunder.

▲ If you open a window or go on a porch, you can smell the air as it fills with rain.

▲ Look at the water on trees and grass and see how it glistens.

▲ Notice the puddles that the rain makes.

I'm Looking Out the Window
●●●●●●●●●●●●●●●●●●●●●●●●●

Encourages observation skills

▲ Sing the following song to the tune of "I'm Following the Leader":

> I'm looking out the window, the window, the window.
> I'm looking out the window,
> And this is what I see.

▲ Say, "I see a _____." Say words that your child will recognize immediately. For example, "I see a tree."

▲ Sing the song again and on the last line sing, "And this is what (child's name) sees."

▲ Help your child either say a word or point to something and then sing the song again, putting in the object that your child named.

Balloon Fun

Teaches about propulsion

▲ Take a half gallon milk carton and cut it in half the long way. It should lay flat on the table.

▲ Poke a hole in the middle of the carton.

▲ Blow up a balloon and put the end of the balloon through the hole.

▲ When you let go of the balloon, the carton will move as the air empties out of the balloon.

▲ This is great fun to do over and over.

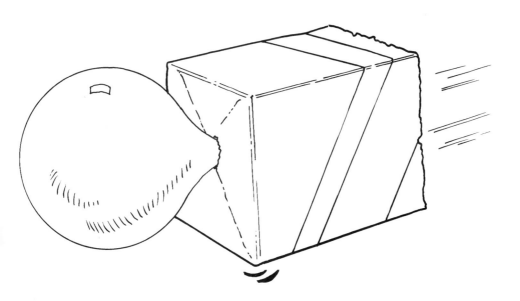

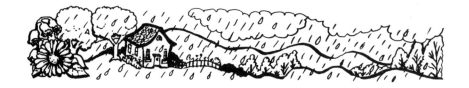

Mirror, Mirror
•••••••••••••••••••••••••••

Teaches about parts of the body

▲ Looking in the mirror fascinates young children. This is a good game to help her learn the different parts of her body.
▲ Say to your child, "Mirror, mirror, on the wall. Who's the finest girl (boy) of all? Can you find your nose?"
▲ When your child sees herself touching her nose, she will be delighted.
▲ Continue naming different parts of the body.

Learning about Senses
•••••••••••••••••••••••••••

Develops self-esteem

▲ Show your child how different parts of his body can do wonderful things.
▲ Act out the following rhyme:

> *You have eyes that can see many things. (point out objects)*
> *You have a nose that can smell many things. (sniff)*
> *You have ears that can hear many things. (make sounds)*
> *You have a mouth that can taste many things. (taste something)*
> *You are special and unique.*

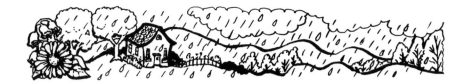

Do What I Do
●●●●●●●●●●●●●●●●●●●●●●●●●●●●●●●

Develops self-esteem

▲ Young children enjoy imitating adults. Giving your child jobs to do will give him a feeling of accomplishment.
▲ Suggestions include:

    ✓ Putting papers in a recycling basket
    ✓ Mixing and stirring a recipe
    ✓ Putting silverware in a dishwasher
    ✓ Putting clothes away in a drawer

Looking at Oranges
●●●●●●●●●●●●●●●●●●●●●●●●●●●●●●

Encourages sensory development

▲ Looking at an orange can be a fascinating experience for your child.
▲ Peel it first, then let your child feel and smell the peel.
▲ Separate the orange into sections and count the sections as you separate them.
▲ Show your child the seeds inside the orange.
▲ Smell the orange and eat it.
▲ Your child has used several senses—seeing, smelling, feeling and tasting.
▲ Repeat with other fruits or vegetables.

STUCK INSIDE GAMES

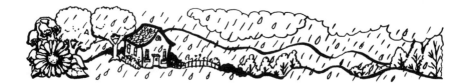

Something Sweet
● ●

Teaches sensory development

▲ Sit down with your child and show her a lemon.

▲ Tell her about the lemon and let her hold it and smell it.

▲ Cut the lemon in half and let her hold it and smell it again.

▲ Squeeze the juice into a glass.

▲ Taste the lemon juice and tell her it is sour.

▲ Let her taste the lemon juice. Say the word, "Sour" again.

▲ Add water and sugar to the juice to make lemonade.

▲ Now taste it and say the word, "Sweet." Let her taste the lemonade and say the word, "Sweet" again.

Blocks and Boxes
● ●

Develops thinking skills

▲ You will need a small box and a block to play this game.

▲ Ask your child to put the block in the box and then take it out of the box.

▲ Then put the block over the box, beside the box, behind the box. These words can be confusing, especially to a very young child. It's best to start with two directions and add others as your child understands the concepts.

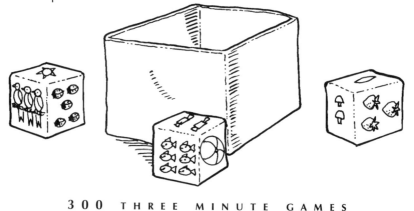

Looking for Treasures
●●●●●●●●●●●●●●●●●●●●●●●●

Enhances thinking skills

▲ This is a game to stimulate your child's thinking.
▲ You will need a few colored, plastic eggs (or any other colorful objects) for this game.
▲ Hide the eggs in several places in the same room (always leave part of the egg visible).
▲ Ask your child to find the eggs.
▲ Give him hints as to where the eggs are.
▲ Praise him when he finds one.
▲ After you have played this game a few times, ask your child to hide the eggs and let you find them.

Let's Pretend
●●●●●●●●●●●●●●●●●●●●●●●●

Teaches thinking skills

▲ Pretending teaches the difference between reality and fantasy.
▲ Tell your child you are going to pretend to eat an ice cream cone.
▲ Pretend to lick the ice cream, make comments about the taste and chew the cone.
▲ Ask him to copy you and pretend to eat an ice cream cone.
▲ Pretend to do things that are familiar to your child. For example, brushing teeth, drinking milk, combing hair and blowing out candles on a birthday cake.
▲ Pretending is also a good way to develop your child's imagination.

Boo, Hoo, Hoo!
● ●

Practices thinking skills

▲ You will need a container of plastic animals that your child can identify as you say the rhyme.

> *Boo, hoo, hoo!*
> *Where are you?*
> *I want my cow,*
> *Boo, hoo, hoo!*

▲ Ask your child to find the cow in the container. When he finds it, ask him what sound the cow makes.

▲ This is a good game for learning animal sounds.

▲ You can also play this game to identify colors.

> *Boo, hoo, hoo!*
> *Where are you?*
> *I want red*
> *Boo, hoo, hoo!*

▲ Ask your child to find something red in the container.

▲ Young children love to play this game and say, "Boo, hoo, hoo!"

Stuffed Animal Games

Hold Them High
● ●

Teaches about following directions

▲ Give your child a stuffed animal and ask her to hold the animal high in the air. Say the following poem:

> *Hold your hands up to the sky,*
> *High, high, up to the sky.*
> *Take your tiger (or another animal) and fly high,*
> > *(pretend to fly with stuffed animal)*
> *High, high, in the sky.*

▲ Keep repeating the poem and on the line "Take your tiger and fly high," change the activity. Other suggestions include:

> *Take your tiger and give her a kiss....*
> *Take your tiger and turn around....*
> *Take your tiger and bend over....*

Let's Go to the Store
•••••••••••••••••••••••••••••

Develops imagination

▲ I have played this game with many young children, and they love it.

▲ Take a stuffed animal and put it on your head.

▲ Tell your child, "I'm taking rabbit (or another animal) to the store." Wave good-bye and walk to another part of the room.

▲ Drop the stuffed animal from your head to the floor and say, "Here we are at the store."

▲ Pick up the animal, put it on your head and say, "I'm taking rabbit (or another animal) to the park."

▲ Continue playing the game until your child understands it.

▲ Give the animal to your child and ask him to go to the store or to the park with the animal.

Pretending
•••••••••••••••••••••••••••••

Encourages imagination

▲ Sit on the floor with your child and a favorite stuffed animal.

▲ Hold up a saucer and a cup and tell your child the names of each.

▲ Say the following rhyme:

This is my hand. (hold up your hand)
This is my cup. (hold up a cup)
This is the way I lift it up. (lift the cup to your mouth)

▲ Say the poem again but change the last line.

Pour in the milk and drink it up.
(pretend to pour milk and drink it)

▲ Say the poem again and pretend to feed the stuffed animal.

▲ Change the liquid in the cup to water or juice.

Where's the Tiger?

● ●

Teaches about in and out

▲ Take a stuffed tiger (or any stuffed animal) and place it in a large box.
▲ Ask your child to take the tiger out of the box.
▲ Ask your child to put the tiger in the box.
▲ Keep asking your child to put the tiger in and take it out of the box.
▲ Sing the following song to the tune of "London Bridge":

> *Put the tiger in the box*
> *One, two, three,*
> *Fiddle, dee, dee.*
> *Put the tiger in the box*
> *My fair lady.*

> *Take the tiger out of the box*
> *One, two, three,*
> *Fiddle, dee, dee.*
> *Take the tiger out of the box*
> *My fair lady.*

Postcards

●●●●●●●●●●●●●●●●●●●●●●●●●●●●●●●

Develops imagination

▲ Cut up cereal boxes to make postcards.
▲ Tell your child that you are going to write a card to his stuffed animals.
▲ Talk about each animal and ask him what he could say on his postcards. For example, he could tell his teddy bear, "I love you."
▲ Give him a few crayons and ask him to write on the postcard.
▲ Deliver the mail to the teddy bear.
▲ Do this with dolls and other stuffed animals.

Buzzy, Buzzy

●●●●●●●●●●●●●●●●●●●●●●●●●●●●●●●

Enhances language skills

▲ Sing the following song to the tune of "John Brown's Body." Your child will enjoy trying to sing this song.
▲ Ask her to hold her favorite stuffed animal and sing to it.

> *A busy buzzing bumble bee went busily buzzing by.*
> *A busy buzzing bumble bee went busily buzzing by.*
> *A busy buzzing bumble bee went busily buzzing by.*
> *And then he stopped and buzzzzzzzzed. Ouch!*

▲ On the first three lines, make your fingers be bumble bees and buzz all around the stuffed friend.
▲ On the last line, tickle the stuffed friend in the tummy.

Back and Forth
● ●

Practices listening skills

▲ Sit on the floor facing your child.
▲ Explain to your child that the two of you are going to pass the stuffed animal back and forth until the singing (or music if there is another person to play recorded music) stops.
▲ Start singing "The Farmer in the Dell."
▲ As you sing, give the toy to your child and have her give it back to you.
▲ Keep passing the toy back and forth until you stop singing.
▲ It's a good idea to sing at least two lines of the song before you stop.

Body Rhythms

Builds listening skills

▲ Ask your child to nod his head yes and no.
▲ Next, ask him to take his stuffed animal and make the stuffed animal's head nod yes and no.
▲ Ask your child to do the following activities by himself and then have his stuffed animal do the same activity.

✓ Lie on your stomach and kick your legs.
✓ Lie on your back and kick your legs.
✓ Lie on your stomach and kick your legs fast.
✓ Lie on your back and kick your legs slowly.

Where Is the Handkerchief?

Encourages listening skills

▲ Take a favorite stuffed animal and set it on the floor.
▲ Take a handkerchief and put it on the bear's (or another stuffed animal's) head. Tell your child, "The handkerchief is on the bear's head."
▲ Give the handkerchief to your child and ask her to put the handkerchief on the bear's head.
▲ Take the handkerchief and put it on the bear's back.
▲ Ask your child to put the handkerchief on the bear's back.
▲ Continue naming different places for the handkerchief to go.

Sing Like the Animals
●●●●●●●●●●●●●●●●●● ● ● ● ● ● ● ● ● ● ●

Develops listening skills

▲ Take a stuffed animal and talk about the sound that it makes.
▲ Sing a song using that sound.
▲ For example, a duck would sing a song to the tune of "Mary Had a Little Lamb" using the words "quack, quack."
▲ Other song ideas include: "Twinkle, Twinkle, Little Star," "The Farmer in the Dell," "Humpty Dumpty," "Row, Row, Row Your Boat" and "London Bridge."

Head and Shoulders
●●●●●●●●●●●●●●●● ● ● ● ● ● ● ● ● ● ● ●

Teaches about parts of the body

▲ Take a stuffed animal and let your child identify different parts of the stuffed animal's body.
▲ Ask her where are the animal's head, shoulders, knees, toes, eyes, ears, mouth and nose.
▲ When she can tell you where each of those parts of the body are on her favorite stuffed animal, sing the following song to the tune of "London Bridge."
▲ Let her touch the parts of the stuffed animal's body as you sing the song.

> *Head and shoulders, knees and toes*
> *Knees and toes, knees and toes*
> *Head and shoulders, knees and toes*
> *Eyes and ears and mouth and nose.*

Ten Little Fingers

● ●

Teaches about parts of the body

▲ Sit with your child and talk about the different parts of the body.

▲ Talk about fingers, toes, eyes, nose, cheeks, chin and mouth.

▲ Then say the following poem and touch each part of the body as you say the words:

> *Ten little fingers,*
> *Ten little toes,*
> *Two little eyes and*
> *One little nose.*
> *Two little cheeks,*
> *One little chin and*
> *One little mouth where the food goes in!*

▲ Try playing the game with a stuffed animal. This may be more challenging for your child.

Top and Bottom

● ●

Teaches about spatial concepts

▲ Take one of your child's stuffed animals and put it on top of your head.
▲ Tell your child, "The bunny is on the top of my head."
▲ Give the toy to your child and ask her to put the bunny on the top of her head.
▲ Take the stuffed animal and put it on the top of something else like a table, a chair, a counter.
▲ Each time that you put the toy on top of something, give it to your child and encourage her to do the same.
▲ When you feel that your child understands the concept of "top," repeat the game using "bottom."
▲ When talking about both "top" and "bottom" a child loves to put a stuffed animal on her head (top) and then let it fall to the floor (bottom).

Talk to the Animals

● ●

Develops thinking skills

▲ Take two stuffed animals and put them together in a chair.
▲ Talk to the animals and call them by name. If they don't have names, give them names.
▲ Say, "Hello Henry, would you like (child's name) to give you a hug?"
▲ Ask your child to pick up the correct animal and give it a hug.
▲ Continue giving your child different suggestions to do with his stuffed animals. Use the animal's name if it has one.
▲ Here are other suggestions:

✓ Put the animal on your head.
✓ Shake your animal back and forth.
✓ Put the animal behind you.

Showing Teddy

Develops thinking skills

▲ Go for a walk around your house with your child and his favorite stuffed animal.
▲ Ask your child to show teddy different things in a room.
▲ If you are in the kitchen, say, "(Child's name), would you show teddy the refrigerator?"
▲ Name objects in a room that your child knows.
▲ Your child will delight in demonstrating his knowledge.
▲ This game also encourages language skills.

Teddy Is Big!

Promotes thinking skills

▲ Show your child how a magnifying glass works.
▲ This game is great fun with your favorite stuffed animal.
▲ Ask your child to look at lamb's (or another stuffed animal's) ear.
▲ Hold the magnifying glass to lamb's ear and look again.
▲ Talk about what you see through the magnifying glass.
▲ A magnifying glass is so fascinating that your child may want to look at everything using the magnifying glass.

STUFFED ANIMAL GAMES

Pretending
● ●

Improves thinking skills

▲ Tell your child that it's time for lion (or another stuffed animal) to eat lunch.

▲ Let your child pretend to feed lion. Encourage him to talk about what food lion is eating.

▲ Tell your child, "Now, it's time for lion to take a nap."

▲ You will find that many of the words and actions that you do with your child will be repeated as he takes care of his lion.

▲ When a child can copy someone else's actions, it means that he has internalized the concept.

Drawing Fun
● ●

Enhances thinking skills

▲ Use a piece of paper large enough to draw an outline of your child's favorite teddy or stuffed animal.

▲ Ask your child to place the animal on the paper.

▲ Draw an outline of the animal.

▲ Talk about where the different parts of the body are in the picture, such as the legs or the head.

▲ Let your child color and draw on this outline.

▲ You can also draw an outline of your child.

A Singing Game

Practices thinking skills

▲ Your child probably has several stuffed animals.

▲ There are many wonderful songs that are associated with stuffed animals.

▲ Choose two or three toys and line them up next to one another.

▲ Sing a song about one of the toys to your child and ask her to go and get that toy.

▲ An example is singing the song, "Teddy Bear, Teddy Bear" and asking your child to get the teddy bear.

▲ Ask your child to hold the stuffed friend. Sing the song again with your child.

▲ Suggestions include:

✓ Squirrel—"Gray Squirrel"
✓ Horse—"The Old Gray Mare"
✓ Dog—"B-I-N-G-O" and "Oh Where, Oh Where Has My Little Dog Gone?"
✓ Duck—"Five Little Ducks"
✓ Rabbit—"Little Rabbit Foo Foo"
✓ Teddy Bear—"The Bear Went Over the Mountain"
✓ Elephant—"One Elephant"
✓ Monkey—"Three Little Monkeys"
✓ Cat—"Three Little Kittens"
✓ Lamb—"Mary Had a Little Lamb"

This Is the Way

Develops thinking skills

▲ When a child can repeat an action that he has seen someone else do, it means that he has internalized the concept.

▲ Take your child's favorite stuffed animal and do the actions in the following song.

▲ Sing the song to the tune of "Mulberry Bush."

> *This is the way we wash our face, wash our face, wash our face.*
> *(pretend to wash the stuffed animal's face)*
> *This is the way we wash our face*
> *On a cold and frosty morning.*
>
> *This is the way we drink our milk....*
> *(pretend to give the stuffed animal milk)*
>
> *This is the way we jump up and down....*
> *(move the stuffed animal up and down)*

▲ Help your child think of all the things he can do with his stuffed animal.

Thinking
Games

I WONDER...!

Looking at Rocks

Teaches about big and little

▲ Fill a box with rocks that are two distinct sizes, big and little.
Note: Do not use pebbles since they can pose a choking hazard.
▲ Look at the rocks with your child and use the words "big" and "little."
▲ Put the rocks into two separate boxes. One box for the big rocks and one box for the little rocks.
▲ Help your child separate the rocks into two groups of rocks—big and little.
▲ As your child grows older, she will make other comparisons of big and little.

How Tall?

Teaches about comparisons

▲ Many adults play a game with children asking them, "How big are you?" The answer children often give is, "So big."
▲ This game is an extension of the game about big and little.
▲ Walk around the house with your child and talk about what is taller than he is and what is not taller than he is.
▲ Ask, "Are you taller than the table?" Stand next to the table and show him how to compare his height to the height of the table.
▲ Now, tell him to ask and answer the question, "Am I taller than the table?"
▲ Ask your child to stand next to a chair and ask, "Are you taller than the chair?"
▲ Encourage your child to play this game with his stuffed animals.

Filling Bagels

●●●●●●●●●●●●●●●●●●●●●●●●

Promotes coordination

▲ Put a whole bagel on the table.
▲ Give your child a selection of small food items, such as dry cereal, small chunks of cheese, carrot sticks and raisins. Ask your child to fill the center of the bagel.
▲ The fun of this game is to fill the hole in the center of the bagel and then to empty it.
▲ Of course, it's also fun to eat the food items at the end of the game.

Inside and Outside

●●●●●●●●●●●●●●●●●●●●●●●●

Encourages coordination

▲ Take string and make a circle on the floor.
▲ Stand inside the circle and then jump outside the circle.
▲ Ask your child to jump inside the circle and then, ask your child to jump outside the circle.
▲ Put your foot in the circle. Take your foot out of the circle. Encourage your child to do the same.
▲ Put your hand in the circle. Take your hand out of the circle. Encourage your child to do the same.
▲ Continue putting different parts of the body in and out of the circle.

THINKING GAMES

The Alphabet Game
●●●●●●●●●●●●●●●●●●●●●●●●●

Teaches letter recognition

▲ Learning to recognize letters is an important prereading skill.
▲ Your child will love looking for letters wherever you go.
▲ To begin, choose a letter that is easy to identify like an "M" or an "O".
▲ Print the letter for your child and tell her the name of the letter.
▲ Look for that letter in books, magazines, on labels and on cereal boxes.
▲ When you ride in the car, look for that letter on street signs and billboards.
▲ Wherever you travel, look for the letter.
▲ When you feel your child knows the letter, choose a new letter.

Hands and Feet
●●●●●●●●●●●●●●●●●●●●●●●●

Develops matching skills

▲ Draw an outline of your child's hand and foot on a piece of paper.
▲ Cut out the hand and foot and place them on the floor. You might want to glue them to a piece of cardboard.
▲ Ask your child to put her hand on the cutout of the hand.
▲ Ask your child to put her foot on the cutout of the foot.
▲ You can give your child crayons or markers and let her decorate the hand and foot.
▲ In six months or a year cut out your child's hand and foot again. Compare the two sets of hands and feet.

How? Why? I Wonder... Why? How? I WONDER!... I Wonder...

Birthday Fun

● ●

Teaches about numbers

▲ Birthdays are very special to everyone and especially to young children.
▲ Young children enjoy holding up their fingers when asked, "How old are you?"
▲ Hold up one finger and ask your child to do the same. Ask your child, "Are you one?"
▲ Shake your head and say in a very dramatic voice, "No, no, no!"
▲ Hold up seven fingers and ask your child to do the same. Then, ask the question again, "Are you seven?"
▲ Continue playing the game and when you come to the correct number, say, "Yes, yes, yes, hooray!"

Card Game

● ●

Develops observation skills

▲ Show your child a deck of cards. Choose one or two of the pictures for him to recognize, for example, the king and queen.
▲ Deal three or four of the same cards to you and your child. The cards should include one of the pictures that your child recognizes.
▲ Pick the queen from your pile and ask your child to find the matching card.
▲ As your child gets older and understands this game, add the number cards to the game.
▲ You can also match the colors of the cards.

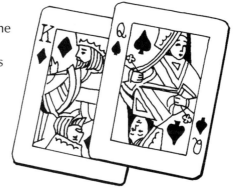

What Can You Do?
●●●●●●●●●●●●●●●●●●●●●●●●●●●●●●

Teaches about parts of the body

▲ This game emphasizes one part of the body at a time. The idea is to think of many things to do with that body part. For example, with hands, you can shake, wave, clap, snap, tickle.
▲ Here are additional ideas

✓ Blink your eyes...and other things eyes can do
✓ Move your ears...and other things ears can do
✓ Puff your cheeks...and other things cheeks can do
✓ Open your mouth...and other things mouths can do

Get the Toy
●●●●●●●●●●●●●●●●●●●●●●●●●●●

Promotes problem-solving skills

▲ Ask your child to retrieve a toy under a chair.
▲ Plan it so that he will not be able to reach it with his hands.
▲ Give him a wooden spoon or another tool to retrieve the toy and show him how to use it.
▲ Try this game another day and see if he remembers to use the spoon to retrieve the toy.
▲ This game helps develop creativity as well as problem-solving skills.

Get the Toy Again

Practices problem-solving skills

▲ This is another toy game.

▲ Tie a string to a favorite toy.

▲ Place the toy out of the reach of the child, but place the string that is attached to the toy within the reach of the child.

▲ If she does not use the string to retrieve the toy, show her how to pull the string to retrieve the toy.

Silverware

Teaches sorting skills

▲ Take spoons and forks and put them on the table.

▲ Mix them up.

▲ Ask your child to give you a spoon. Put it down away from the rest of the silverware.

▲ Ask your child to give you a fork. Put it down in another place.

▲ As your child gives you spoons and forks, sort them into groups of spoons and forks.

▲ Ask your child to put the spoons with the other spoons and the forks with the other forks.

▲ After your child has practiced sorting spoons and forks, ask him to put the silverware away after meals.

Apples

Enhances thinking skills

▲ Say the following poem and do the actions:

> *There's an apple up in the apple tree. (point up high)*
> *How can we get it? Well, let's see.*
> *We can climb up the tree and pick it off. (pretend to climb)*
> *We can shake the tree and drop it off. (pretend to shake tree)*
> *What shall we do? (ask your child to decide and act out the idea*
>   *that she suggests)*
> *What a good idea, yum, yum, yum! (pretend to eat the apple)*

Boxes and More Boxes

Develops thinking skills

▲ This game requires the advance preparation of gathering empty boxes.
▲ Cereal boxes, shoe boxes and gift boxes are good boxes to use in this game.
▲ When you think that you have saved enough boxes (no more than ten for a young child), put them on the floor.
▲ Sit on the floor with your child and just watch her experiment with stacking the boxes.
▲ She will quickly learn that the larger ones go on the bottom.
▲ Make suggestions about the boxes to stimulate her imagination.
▲ Boxes can be houses, boats, telephones, hiding places for toys.

I WONDER...

The Fruit Song
• •

Develops thinking skills

▲ Put three kinds of fruit on the table and name them. With young children start with only two fruits.

▲ Let your child touch each one as you name it or ask your child to name the fruit with you.

▲ Make up a song to the tune of "Mary Had a Little Lamb" using the names of the fruit in the song.

> *(Child's name) had a little apple, little apple, little apple.*
> *(Child's name) had a little apple,*
> *And it was delicious.*
>
> *She also had a little grape....*
> *She also had a little strawberry....*

▲ Keep singing about each fruit and when you have named all of the fruits, sing

> *(Child's name) has a fruit salad, fruit salad, fruit salad.*
> *(Child's name) has a fruit salad,*
> *And she ate it all.*

T H I N K I N G   G A M E S

Where's the Nut?

Develops thinking skills

▲ Put out two small paper drinking cups. Turn them both upside down.
▲ Show your child a whole walnut and let him watch as you put the walnut under one of the cups.
▲ Ask him, "Where is the walnut?"
▲ If he doesn't understand, lift up the correct cup and say, "Here it is."
▲ Keep playing until he understands. When he understands the game, add another cup.
▲ Let your child hide the walnut and you try to find it.

What Do You Do With That?

Encourages thinking skills

▲ Young children understand many words, recognize many people and can do many tasks.
▲ This game presents information that your child may already know in a different way.
▲ Look at a magazine together. Instead of naming the picture in the magazine, pose a question. For example, "What do you do with that red, round thing?" or "What can the thing with a tail do?"
▲ Choose familiar pictures but ask about them in a different way.

Transition
Games

Crawling Caterpillars
●●●●●●●●●●●●●●●●●●●●●●●●●●●●●●●

Promotes coordination

▲ This game is more meaningful if you have looked at pictures of caterpillars or observed them moving before you play the game.

▲ Get on the floor with your child. Move on your tummy like a caterpillar.

▲ Say the following poem as you crawl like a caterpillar:

> *Caterpillar, caterpillar*
> *Crawl, crawl, crawl*
> *Caterpillar, caterpillar*
> *Crawl to the wall.*

▲ Do the action stated in the poem and try to crawl to the wall.

▲ Keep repeating the poem with a different last line. Crawl to the chair or crawl to the door.

▲ Ask your child, "Where do you crawl, Mr. (or Ms.) Caterpillar?"

▲ Once you have played this game, you can use it successfully to encourage your child to move from one activity to another or from one room to another.

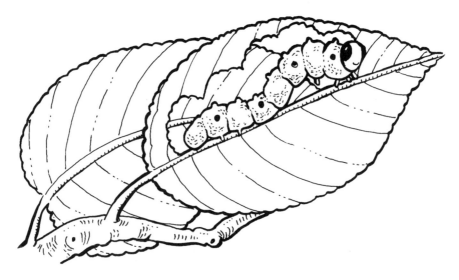

The Colored Circle Game

Teaches color recognition

▲ This game makes transitions of moving from one room to another room easier because the child is looking for something.

▲ Cut out circles large enough for your child to hold and to be able to find easily.

▲ If you want your child to go to another room, put a colored circle in that room for your child to find.

▲ Give your child a matching colored circle and tell her that you are going to look for another circle, for example, in the bathroom.

▲ This game is fun to play and will encourage your child to go to the room you choose.

This Is the Way

Enhances coordination

▲ Moving your child from one activity to another may be difficult.

▲ Getting ready for a bath, for a meal or to go outside can sometimes be frustrating for both of you.

▲ Singing is a gentle and fun way to encourage your child to transition to another activity.

▲ Sing the following to the tune of "Here We Go 'Round the Mulberry Bush":

> *This is the way I like to jump*
> *Like to jump, like to jump.*
> *This is the way I like to jump*
> *Off to the bathtub.*
>
> *This is the way I like to creep...*
> *This is the way I like to dance...*
> *This is the way I like to march...*

Scarf Walks
● ●

Encourages creativity

▲ Moving from one room to another is great fun when you use a scarf.
▲ You hold one end and give your child the other end.
▲ Tell your child in advance where you will be going with the scarf.
▲ Announce, "Ready, set, go!" Start walking toward your destination.
▲ Walk in different ways, such as slowly, on your tiptoes, teeny steps.
▲ Your child will copy you and have a wonderful time.
▲ Encourage your child to hold onto the scarf as you walk.

Mr. Sun
● ●

Teaches language skills

▲ This is a good poem to say to your child when she is getting up in the morning or after a nap. It is also an enjoyable way to transition from sleeping to the next activity.

> *Good morning, Mister Sun*
> *I hope you're feeling fine.*
> *The day has just begun*
> *So shine, shine, shine.*
> *Good morning, good morning*
> *Good morning, Mr. Sun.*

▲ Substitute your child's name for Mr. Sun.

Wake Up and Sing
● ●

Teaches language skills

▲ This is another poem to do first thing in the morning (or after a nap) to transition from waking up in the morning to starting the day.

> *I wake up in the morning*
> *And the very first thing*
> *I get up from my bed*
> *And I sing, sing, sing!*

▲ Pick a song that your child likes and sing it.

Talk Like the Animals
● ●

Promotes listening skills

▲ Young children love to make animal sounds. They love to answer the question, "What does the cow say?"
▲ When you would like your child to change to another activity, making animal sounds is a helpful tool.
▲ Instead of saying, "Let's put away the toys," say, "The cow wants to put away the toys."
▲ As you say, "Moo, moo" start picking up toys and soon your child will imitate both what you are saying and what you are doing.
▲ You can try this idea in other transitional situations including:

✓ Time to eat a meal
✓ Time to get in the car
✓ Time to go to bed

Move Like the Wind

● ●

Develops listening skills

▲ Say the following poem.

> Oh, the wind blows east. (blow and say "whooo")
> Oh, the wind blows west. (blow and say "whooo")
> The wind blows (child's name) right down to town.

▲ Repeat this poem and let the wind blow your child into a change of activity. For example, "The wind blew (child's name) right into the kitchen."

▲ As you leave one activity to go to another, blow like the wind as you make the change.

Touching

● ●

Improves listening skills

▲ Give your child instructions to touch different parts of her body to objects in the room.

> ✓ Touch your nose to the chair.
> ✓ Touch your head to the wall.

▲ After you have played the game a few times, you can use it as a transition game.

> ✓ Touch your toe to the bathtub. (when it's bath time)
> ✓ Touch your elbow to the sink. (when it's time to wash hands)

We Are Going to the Kitchen
●●●●●●●●●●●●●●●●●●●●●●●●●●●●

Practices listening skills

▲ If you want your child to come to the kitchen, sing the following song to the tune of "She'll Be Comin' 'Round the Mountain":

> *We are going to the kitchen right away.*
> *We are going to the kitchen right away.*
> *We are going to the kitchen,*
> *We are going to the kitchen,*
> *We are going to the kitchen right away.*

▲ If you want your child to go to the bathtub, sing

> *We are going to the bathtub right away....*

It's All in the Timing
●●●●●●●●●●●●●●●●●●●●●●●●●

Teaches listening skills

▲ Moving from one activity to another can be frustrating for the adult and for the child.
▲ Since young children do not understand time, if you tell them that in five minutes it will be time to stop, they may not understand.
▲ Instead, use a timer as a warning signal to get ready to make a change.
▲ After the timer beeps or rings, you can give your child directions for the transition, such as one of the activities in this chapter.

Finding Two

● ●

Teaches about numbers

▲ Take your child's hand and put her hand on each of your ears. As you do this, count, "One, two." Continue with your thumbs, your hands and your feet.

▲ Walk around the room with your child and find two of anything as you count, "One, two."

▲ Ask your child to hold up two fingers and count them.

▲ This is an excellent transition activity. Look for two of anything in the room that you would like your child to move toward.

Lift Off!

● ●

Teaches about numbers

▲ Ask your child to sit on the floor and kneel behind him.

▲ Start counting backward from ten as you slowly lift him to his feet and then into the air.

▲ When you get to zero, say, "Lift off," and hold him high in the air.

▲ Now "Lift off" to another activity, such as bath time or eating lunch.

Travel Trail

● ●

Teaches observation skills

▲ This is a good transition game and will increase your child's observation skills at the same time.

▲ Tear up pieces of colored paper. The pieces should all be the same color.

▲ When you want your child to go to a different room, make a trail of the colored paper.

▲ Help your child follow the trail and pick up the paper as you go along.

▲ Praise your child at the end of the trail.

Waiting Games

Copycat
· ·

Develops an awareness of others

▲ Ask your child to copy your actions.

    ✓ Open and close your fist
    ✓ Put your hands together and shake them
    ✓ Blink your eyes
    ✓ Cough
    ✓ Yawn
    ✓ Bend your index finger
    ✓ Tap your fingers on your opposite shoulder

▲ Keep adding new actions to this list.

One Foot
· ·

Teaches balance

▲ Waiting with a young child can be frustrating especially if you are in a situation where she needs to stay in a confined space.

▲ Balancing on one foot is a good game for a situation like this.

▲ Tell your child to try and stand on one foot while you sing a song. Sing a familiar song like "Old MacDonald Had a Farm."

▲ Take turns or do it together and keep changing the song while you see how long you can stand on one foot.

Find the Color

Enhances color recognition

▲ This is a good game to play in a large area, such as an airport or train station where your child can move around.

▲ Say the following rhyme:

> *Many colors, many hues*
> *Which bright color shall I choose?*
> *I choose red!*

▲ Holding your child's hand, walk around the area and find things that are red.

▲ Each time you see something red, say the rhyme, walk toward the red object and touch it.

▲ Continue the game using other colors in the rhyme.

Green Light, Go!

Promotes color recognition

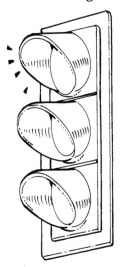

▲ Car trips provide an opportunity to learn about colors.
▲ Each time you come to a stop light, point it out to your child.
▲ Each time the light turns green, say, "Green light, go!"
▲ Soon your child will be saying, "Go" when it is time to go.
▲ At red lights, you say, "Red light, stop!"

Here Is a Man (or Woman)

Develops coordination

▲ Hold up the index finger of each hand.
▲ One finger is the bridge and the other finger is the man.
▲ Say the following rhyme to your child:

> Here is the bridge. (move one finger)
> Here is the man. (move the other finger)
> He wants to go over the bridge.
> Do you think he can?

▲ Move one finger over the other.
▲ Help your child play the game with his fingers.
▲ After you have played the game a few times, add other ideas. For example, the man wants to go under the bridge, on top of the bridge, jump on the bridge and sleep on the bridge.

300 THREE MINUTE GAMES

Peas Porridge
•••••••••••••••••••••••••

Develops coordination

▲ This is a good game if you are waiting in a confined area where it is difficult to let your child move around.
▲ Sit facing your child. Say the following poem as you clap each other's hands.
▲ It's easier for young children if you hold your hands steady as they clap their hands on your hands.

> *Peas porridge hot,*
> *Peas porridge cold,*
> *Peas porridge in the pot*
> *Nine days old.*

▲ After you say, "Nine days old" hold your nose and say, "Phew!"

Silly Clown
•••••••••••••••••••••••••

Improves coordination

▲ Simple fingerplays are good for waiting in an office or in a line at a store.
▲ Move your index finger as you say the following poem:

> *I'm a silly little clown, (wiggle finger back and forth)*
> *And I move up and down. (bend finger down)*
> *I can move my finger up. (straighten finger)*
> *I can move my finger down. (bend finger down)*
> *I'm a silly little clown. (wiggle finger back and forth)*
> *I'm a silly little clown.*

▲ Try using a different finger as you say the poem again.

Snail, Snail

● ●

Encourages coordination

▲ Fingerplays are good to use when you are in a waiting situation. Young children like to do them over and over.
▲ Make a fist and tuck your thumb inside.
▲ Hold up your index finger and your little finger to make the horns.
▲ Say the following rhyme as you wiggle your fingers (horns):

> Snail, snail, put out your horns,
> I'll give you some peas and corn.

▲ Help your child make his fingers like yours.

Building a Chimney

● ●

Teaches counting skills

▲ Put your fingertips together to make a pretend chimney.
▲ As you say the following poem, raise your "chimney" slowly as you count:

> I'm going to build a chimney
> Very, very, high.
> I'll build it up with bricks
> And it will touch the sky,
> 1, 2, 3, 4, 5.

▲ How high you count will depend on the age of the child.
▲ Another idea for this game, is to change the word "bricks" to other words that capture you child's imagination, for example, gumdrops.

Counting to Ten

•••••••••••••• • • • • • • • • • • •

Develops counting skills

▲ Count with your child in different ways.

    ✓ Count softly and say ten in a big voice.
    ✓ Count loudly and say ten in a soft voice.
    ✓ Hold up your fingers as you count.
    ✓ Count and do an action on number ten. You can clap, jump, hop
       and stomp your feet.
    ✓ March in place as you count.
    ✓ Close your eyes as you count and open them on ten.

▲ With very young children count to three. Gradually work up to the
   number ten with older children.

This Old Man

● ●

Teaches counting skills

▲ "This Old Man" is a great song to sing while waiting in a doctor's office, after ordering food in a restaurant and in many other waiting situations.

> *This old man, he played one.*
> *He played knick knack on my thumb. (kiss child's thumb)*
> *With a knick knack paddy whack*
> *Give a dog a bone.*
> *This old man went rolling home. (take child's fists and roll them over each other)*
>
> *This old man, he played two.... (touch child's shoe and continue with the rest of the song)*
>
> *This old man, he played three.... (touch child's knee and continue with the rest of the song)*

▲ Keep counting as high as you think your child can remember.

> *...four...door....*
> *...five...hive....*
> *...six...sticks....*
> *...seven...up to heaven....*
> *...eight...gate....*
> *...nine...spine....*
> *...ten...all again....*

Art in the Car
● ●

Enhances creativity

▲ If you find yourself having to wait in traffic quite often, this activity is just the one for you.

▲ Take a soft three ring binder and fill it with plain white paper.

▲ Attach a resealable plastic bag to the inside of the binder and keep two or three nontoxic markers in the bag. Keep these in your car.

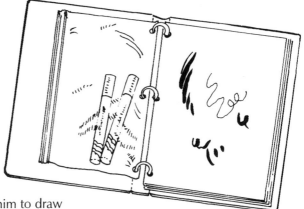

▲ Give the markers and paper to your child and encourage him to draw pictures.

My Hands
● ●

Encourages creativity

▲ Think of all the things to do with hands.

✓ Look at them.
✓ Bend the wrist in different ways, such as down, up, around in a circle.
✓ Shake, wiggle, snap, open and close fingers.
✓ Hold hands together.
✓ Count the fingers.

▲ Continue with more ideas of what to do with hands.

Fast and Slowly

Teaches about fast and slow

▲ The following ideas are helpful when you are in a waiting situation.

▲ Say this poem and do the actions.

> Clap, clap, clap your hands
> As slowly as you can.
> Clap, clap, clap your hands
> As quickly as you can.

▲ Continue doing other actions slowly and quickly.

> Shake, shake, shake your hands....
> Roll, roll, roll your hands....
> Rub, rub, rub your hands....
> Wiggle, wiggle, wiggle your fingers....
> Pound, pound, pound your fists....
> Kick, kick, kick your feet....

Bzzz

Teaches fun

▲ Sit your child on your lap and say the following poem:

> The bumble bee went to the barn. (gently poke your finger into
>   child's tummy)
> With a shovel under his arm.
> The shovel fell and the little bee went
> Bzzzzzzzzzzz. (tickle your child all over)

Let's Sing
• •

Develops language skills

▲ Make a list of familiar songs that your child knows and keep it with you when you are traveling.

▲ When you have an unexpected waiting time, pull out the list and start singing.

▲ The following are songs that young children enjoy:

"Old MacDonald Had a Farm"
"Twinkle, Twinkle, Little Star"
"The Muffin Man"
"The ABC Song" (same melody as "Twinkle, Twinkle, Little Star")
"The Wheels on the Bus"
"Where Is Thumbkin?"
"Happy Birthday" (even when it's not a child's birthday)

▲ If desired, change the words of the song to fit the occasion. For example, if you are going to the mall, sing "Old MacDonald went to he mall." Continue the song naming things your child will see at the mall.

Rhyming Words

● ●

Encourages language skills

▲ Young children love to hear rhyming words and it is a fun way to improve language skills.

▲ While waiting in a car or any other place, make up rhymes.

▲ Accent the rhyming words to emphasize the sound of the word.

> *My hat is BLUE.*
> *It fell on my SHOE.*
> *What shall I DO?*
> *Toodle-OOOH!*

Did You Hear That?

● ●

Promotes listening skills

▲ Waiting in the doctor's office? Try this game to pass the time.

▲ Ask your child to close his eyes.

▲ Make a sound with your hands.

▲ Ask him to tell you what you did. If he doesn't have the language to say the words, ask him to show you what you did.

▲ Try several different kinds of sounds.

> ✓ Clap your hands
> ✓ Snap your fingers
> ✓ Hum
> ✓ Knock on a surface
> ✓ Make a kissing sound with your lips

I See a ....

Teaches observation skills

▲ This is a good waiting game to play in a restaurant.
▲ Say, "I see a ...." Name something that is nearby and can be touched. For example, if you are sitting at a table, you can say, "Napkin."
▲ Ask your child to touch the napkin.
▲ Continue the game, naming silverware, glasses and anything else within reach.

Amble Bamble

Develops observation skills

▲ Take a small toy and put it in your hand.
▲ Be sure your child knows which hand the toy is in.
▲ Put both hands behind your back and say the following poem:

> *Amble, bamble, biddely boo*
> *Which hand has a toy for you?*

▲ Ask your child to choose the hand with the toy.
▲ This game can also reinforce number concepts by saying to your child, "Which hand is it in, number one or number two?"

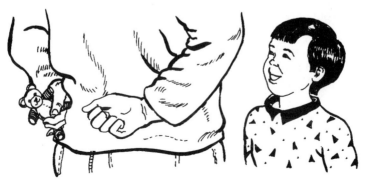

W A I T I N G   G A M E S

Hello, Car

●●●●●●●●●●●●●●●●●●●●●●●●●●●

Improves observation skills

▲ This is a good game to play if you are waiting in traffic.
▲ Say the following rhyme:

> *Look out the window,*
> *What do you see?*
> *I see a car*
> *Looking at me.*

▲ Ask your child, "Do you see the car?"
▲ Say, "Hello, car." Ask your child to say, "Hello, car."
▲ Repeat the poem and change the word "car" to something else you can see from the window.
▲ This game diverts your child's attention and at the same time helps her develop observation skills.

Peekaboo

●●●●●●●●●●●●●●●●●●●●●●●●●●●

Teaches about parts of the body

▲ All peekaboo games are good because they teach young children that when something disappears, it will return. And they help pass time enjoyably when waiting.
▲ Sit facing your child.
▲ Take a napkin (or tissue) and cover your nose.
▲ Say, "Peekaboo, peekaboo, I see my nose." Move the napkin away.
▲ Now try to cover your child's nose with the napkin.
▲ Cover different parts of the body.
▲ Give your child the napkin and see if she can play peekaboo covering parts of your body.

Jack-in-the-Box
● ●

Develops a sense of humor

▲ While waiting with your child, here is a fingerplay that will make you both laugh.

▲ Wrap your fingers around the thumb of one hand.

Jack, Jack, where are you?
I can't find you anywhere.
Are you on (child's name) nose?
    (touch child's nose)
Are you on (child's name)
    toes? (touch child's toes)
Jack, Jack, where are you?
There you are! Boo!
    (unwrap your fingers
    and
    stick out your
    thumb)

Shapes
● ●

Enhances shape recognition

▲ The doctor's office usually has many magazines. Help pass the waiting time by playing a shape game as you look through magazines with your child.

▲ Search for one shape at a time. A circle is a good shape with which to begin this game.

▲ Open up a magazine and go through it page by page, looking for circles. You will be amazed at how many circles you will find.

▲ This is an exciting game for a young child.

Where Are Your Eyes?

Promotes thinking skills

▲ No matter where you are waiting, your child will enjoy playing this game.

▲ Ask your child to point to different parts of his body—eyes, nose, tummy, toes.

▲ Now tell him something to do with each part.

    ✓ Wiggle your nose.
    ✓ Pat your tummy.
    ✓ Close your eyes.

Rhyme Time

Encourages thinking skills

▲ Reciting nursery rhymes will bring back memories to you and establish memories for your child.

▲ Nursery rhymes are fun to say anytime and anyplace. A few suggestions include:

"See, Saw, Margery Daw"—outside
"Rub-a-Dub-Dub, Three Men in a Tub"—bathtub
"Little Miss Muffet"—kitchen

▲ Once a child is familiar with a rhyme, start leaving out words (one for each line) and see if she can fill in the word.

▲ Older children enjoy hearing the rhymes mixed up. For example, "Little Jack Horner sat in the corner eating his curds and whey."

Index

●●●●●●●●●●●●●●●●●●●●●●●●●●●●●●